O. E Wesslau

Rational Banking (the Remedy for Depression in Trade)

Versus Bank Monopoly

O. E Wesslau

Rational Banking (the Remedy for Depression in Trade)
Versus Bank Monopoly

ISBN/EAN: 9783337109370

Printed in Europe, USA, Canada, Australia, Japan

Cover: Foto ©Suzi / pixelio.de

More available books at **www.hansebooks.com**

RATIONAL BANKING

(The Remedy for Depression in Trade)

VERSUS

BANK MONOPOLY.

BY

O. E. WESSLAU.

EDITED BY

BANCROFT COOKE.

LONDON:
ELLIOT STOCK, 62, PATERNOSTER ROW, E.C.
1887.

CONTENTS.

PREFACE.

THE endeavour to aid Mr. Wesslau in elaborating the opinions which he has for years held on the subject of this pamphlet has, after due investigation, convinced me of the soundness of his theories, and of the importance of the reforms herein advocated. I trust that however startling the conclusions may appear, an unbiased consideration of the views enunciated may lead all who are interested in economic questions to further the agitation of which this small treatise is intended to be a forerunner.

The extension of the franchise and consequent transference of governing power to the people has struck a fatal blow at legislation in favour of class privileges and monopolies. Much of the beneficent legislation of the last fifty years has consisted in the abrogation of laws passed to protect the interests of the classes in whom the legislative power was formerly vested. For many who have admitted the right of the people to a just share of political power, the growing strength of the democracy has created a fear lest a counter demand should be made, resulting in one-sided legislation of a socialistic nature, designed to gratify unreasonable claims of the masses, who, while conscious of grievances, are ignorant alike of their precise nature and of the true remedies which may and ought to be applied. To militate against the growing tendency to look with favour towards the adoption of communistic theories, it is necessary to crown the progress made towards political equality and freedom of trade by the abolition of all remaining legal inequalities and special monopolies, instead of legislating to mitigate evils which are consequent on their existence.

The depression in trade has caused an outcry on the part of labour against capital. It is obvious that the abundance of capital seeking investment on the one hand, and the large number of unemployed suffering from the want of necessaries, which the co-operation of work and capital produce on the other, is an enigma which the theory of over-production cannot explain. The civilized world suffers from under-consumption and not from over-production. The relative attitudes of capital and labour and their apparent inability to fully co-operate to mutual advantage would point to the conclusion that some artificial obstacle to prosperity must exist. If it can be proved that deterrent legislation is, as in the evil days of protective duties, again responsible, the way may be opened to a new era of national prosperity, to promote which should be the earnest aim of all.

BANCROFT COOKE.

ROWANTREE, BIRKENHEAD,
January 13, 1887.

INTRODUCTION.

THE great prosperity which resulted from the abolition of
the Corn Laws and Protection Duties in Great Britain ought
to have induced the nation to take further steps in the
same direction—viz., towards an entire Free Trade system.
But such has not been the case. We are proud of our so-
called Free Trade, and we seem determined not to re-intro-
duce the same economic follies, at least not in the same
shape ; but during the four decades which have elapsed since
the repeal of the Corn Laws we have advanced very little, if
at all, towards sound national economy.

The reason for this is that we have lost our faith in those
who should lead us on in economic progress—namely, the
political economists.

There are plenty of signs in the world that political
economy has lost whatever small influence it had on men's
minds, both here and abroad. While professors are paid to
teach political economy at the universities, despots and
Parliaments legislate in many countries in direct opposition
to that science, not even heeding the fearful results they
produce by such legislation.

In Great Britain we introduce more and more State interference in our trades; anti-economic measures are eagerly
advocated and easily carried; all political parties favour,
to some extent, State socialism. Political economy is
nowhere, and has been nicknamed 'the dismal science.'
According to popular writers and philanthropists who have
the confidence of the people, political economy has failed
to produce the promised prosperity. They say that it may
enrich the State, but while it tends to make the rich richer
it makes the poor poorer ; that its doctrines are unchristian,
not to say diabolic ; that the survival of the fittest in the
vulgar tongue means something like ' the devil take the
hindmost ;' that applied to human beings this law causes
the most unfit men to survive—namely, the most greedy,
selfish, and cruel; that free demand and supply means
intense competition and mutual extermination ; that the

only remedies political economy proposes consist in miserly
saving, yet keener competition with foreigners, more
machinery, and checks on marriages; that the future which
it points to is dark in the extreme, etc.

As long as these accusations against political economy
are true, it is not surprising that people refuse to accept its
teachings. These would leave them the only choice
between the dreary, helpless, desperate state of things, and
the terribly distasteful remedy of complete socialism. Faith
in Providence and a high destiny for humanity prompt our
leading men to reject the conclusions of the economists, and
to hope for something better. Hence the upholding of our
free economic system against socialistic agitations on the
one hand, and, at the same time, fragmentary experiments
with State socialism on the other.

Dogmatizing in opposition to the nobler instincts of man
has in political economy, as in some other branches of
human knowledge, proved erroneous. Happily for humanity
the dismal theories of the economists will not stand the
tests of either logic or practical experience. The recognised
authorities in economy have started from the unwarranted
supposition that the laws of our country are now, with some
few unimportant exceptions, brought into harmony with
true economy, and that very little remains to be done in
the way of strictly political economic reforms; the dismal
theories are the outcome of the efforts of the economists to
reconcile the existence of a great number of evils, which
they do not perceive to be artificially produced, with their
own theories of the great leading feature in our modern civilization—namely, division of labour. They have assumed
that the tremendous obstacle to the natural organization of
labour which monopoly in banking constitutes is a useful
arrangement, or at least an absolutely necessary evil.

The old fallacy, that banking should not be left free, has
prevailed against the important economic truth that banking, the chief medium of exchange, . ought to be left
entirely free to regulate itself according to circumstances,
and that it can not be subjected to State interference without the gravest consequences to the community.

Banking is, as we shall show in these chapters, the only
possible mechanism of general and free division of labour.
Restricted and vitiated banking therefore means restricted
exchanges, curtailed division of labour, reduced production,
insufficient consumption, reduced wealth, scarcity of work,
and despotism of capital.

It is therefore not surprising that writers who start with the supposition that banking must not be free arrive at very dismal conclusions, and that nations who believe them have to go through dismal experiences.

Political economy, so far, has been an incomplete and inexact science, because the true theories of banking have been unknown. It is therefore quite natural that some of the conclusions of the economists may be wrong, while others are perfectly true, and it would be illogical to reject all indiscriminately. On the contrary, the fact that we have benefited largely from following such teachings of the economists as have stood the test of logical inquiry should commend to us all clearly established economic truths. When true and complete theories of banking have superseded the vague authoritative dogmas which hitherto have held their place, political economy will, we hope, become the trusted guide of legislators.

Though all writers on banking we know are, with one exception, opposed to Free Trade in banking, the general impression which the careful student receives from the perusal of their works is in favour of freedom. They all point to dangers of free note-issuing, which even according to their own reasoning appear impossible. Their unanimous praise of the Scotch free banking, the only real experience the world possesses of free banking, upsets their own theories. Those authors who are aware of these contradictions try to moderate their startling effect by attributing the extraordinary success of the freedom in Scotland to specially favourable circumstances which that country presented during the 150 years the free system was in operation ; but they do not perceive that these favourable circumstances were results which followed, and always must follow, Free Trade in banking.

Several of the best modern economists have either plainly said or hinted that they were well aware of the fact that the true theories of banking were not discovered. Some, like M. Chevalier, leave the all important question of free note-issuing open, simply stating the different theories of the opposing economists. What John Stuart Mill writes amounts to the same : he dismisses the problem with the somewhat curious conclusion, that free note-issuing is very good north of the Tweed, but very bad south of it. Mr. Macleod concludes in favour of the present English system, but he starts from strange premises. He, for instance, confuses the economic term 'capital' with the commercial term 'capital,' and lays down the startling dogma that bankers create capital. If we consider that in economy capital means those material results of previous labour which are consumed in a production, it is not surprising that Mr. Macleod should conclude in favour of monopoly.

Of all economists we know, the Hungarian writer, Horn, who published in Paris, has the clearest and correctest ideas of banking. In his clever book, 'La liberté des Banques,' he throws a great light on the subject. Unfortunately he makes one mistake which has done much to prevent his theories from being accepted. He recommends plurality of State supervised banks where prejudice prohibits entirely free banking. This mistake he made probably because he regarded the intelligently managed 'banqueirs,' establishments in France as the general type of private banks, and did not foresee that following his advice would produce such paper-money-manufacturing usury institutions as the American and Swedish banks.

The objection which might be raised against our theories, that they are more or less in opposition to all writers on banking, loses its importance on examination.

Now there exist in England two influential classes of philanthropic politicians—viz., those who favour benevolent State socialism, and those who uphold rigid political economy, to both of whom this small work more especially appeals. We feared that if it be known to the former that it is written on the lines of strict political economy, and to the latter that we are in opposition to their favourite authorities, neither of them will give our theories the attention we think they deserve. We have therefore been anxious to point out in this short introduction, to the benevolent State socialists, that the teaching of true political economy is not dismal, but that it holds out the brightest prospects to humanity: and to the advocates of political economy, that we differ from their authorities only in points where they differ among themselves, where they are vague, illogical, and in opposition to all practical experience.

If our theories of banking can establish a hearty co-operation between these two classes of philanthropists, now opposing each other, its ultimate object, the adoption of rational banking throughout the Empire, will not be far off.

RATIONAL BANKING

VERSUS

BANK MONOPOLY.

————➤○◄————

I.

THE ORIGIN, THE FUNCTION, AND THE PURPOSE OF BANKING
IN GENERAL.

To form a correct idea of the irresistible and overpowering
influence for good or evil which the banking of a nation
exercises over its prosperity, political power, intelligence,
and morality, we must have a clear knowledge of the circumstances which necessitated its origin, of its function in
the great general co-operation, and especially of the ultimate
aim and end of a good banking system.

Even the best English books on banking, though instructive and technically useful, quite fail to afford this knowledge, and the greatest confusion prevails both in men's
minds and in books respecting the economical theories of
banking.

We must therefore begin with first principles if we wish
to be generally understood.

We shall not begin with the well-known benches of the
Lombard money-changers, from which the word 'bank' is
supposed to be derived, nor describe all the blunders which
have been constantly perpetrated in all countries in connection with coin and banking, from the times of the iron
money of the Spartans to the new German Reichsbank.
All this would not further our object, nor free the reader's
mind from popular prejudices. Also there are many reliable
works on such subjects already extant, and want of space
compels brevity of treatment.

1

But it is necessary to describe briefly how the true economic function of banking, unrecognised or misunderstood, has steadily progressed, notwithstanding all the obstacles which foolish laws, absurd theories, and strong prejudices have thrown in its way, and how we have become possessed of at least some few good methods without understanding the theories of banking. Banking, like most business occupations and institutions, owes its origin to the instinct of self-preservation. Through this instinct the idea of personal property evolved very early. Private property once recognised, common prudence suggested accumulation. Man began to labour to meet not only daily needs, but also future wants. The inducement to labour was strengthened, its value better understood, and how to economise his labour became the chief care of man. Reason and experience pointed to the fact that when labour was divided between two or more workers, it became more productive and at the same time less oppressive than when carried on single-handed. Thus division of labour, or co-operation, was, as it has remained, the fundamental principle of all society.

We cannot dwell as much on the great importance of division of labour as we should wish ; but we may perhaps take for granted that it is generally understood, that without co-operation man would still be in a savage state, and that all wealth and material progress are due to division of labour, either voluntary or compulsory. We shall merely give the outlines of the arguments that lead to this conclusion.

The earth could produce many thousand times more of the things that man requires for his wants, comfort, and enjoyment than are used. A wise Providence has ordained that none of these products, with perhaps the exception of water, should be obtainable or applicable to man's want without labour of some kind. Therefore wealth is originally only obtainable through labour. The better the labour of a community is organized, the more wealthy will that community become ; and as we can do nothing to increase Nature's store, of which there always is enough, it is perfectly correct to say that accumulated labour is wealth. Now the more labour is divided the better organized it is, and the more productive and easy it becomes. Every article of present daily use is an example of the facility with which the most complicated labour is accomplished, when thousands work for each individual and each individual works for many thousands.

Division of labour probably first existed between the members of each family, the men taking such work as suited them best, and assigning special work to the women, sharing the products. When division of labour was extended beyond the family circle, and when patriarchal authority no longer presided over the contribution of labour and division of products, co-operation took necessarily the form of exchange of products. The hunter hunted for the fisherman who fished for the hunter, and they exchanged products.

The great advantages of co-operation by exchange of products induced each family to devote its members to special occupations, according to aptitude, property, or other circumstances. Thus trades and professions originated.

All exchange of products and services were no doubt first effected through direct barter. This kind of traffic had many evident inconveniences, and so indirect exchanges were introduced. Instead of exchanging fish for grain or fruit for tools, goods were first exchanged for some durable article in general demand, which was stored and passed in exchange when the products of others were desired. This originated buying and selling, and gave another considerable impetus to co-operation.

Several kinds of goods, according to time and place, have been used as mediums of exchange, as we use coin. Whatever medium is used for this purpose naturally becomes the measure of value. Gold, silver, and copper were used thus long before they were coined, as they had all the requisite qualities : they were in general demand, were very durable, could be divided to any extent without losing their value, etc.

As these metals easily received and retained impressions, it was found convenient to stamp on each piece, first its weight, and then a name signifying its alloy and weight. Thus coin came into existence.

So far we have reviewed the progress of banking only on the lines of previous writers on the subject, but we can follow them no further. Even here, at the first mention of coin, they, with very few exceptions, make a mistake, or rather accept a fallacy to which they afterwards adhere, and which, leading them into confusion and to conclusions which are opposed to all sound economy and commonsense, adds greatly to the difficulty of their task.

This mistake is the use of such words as ' money ' and ' currency.' These words should never be used by economists, because in reality there is nothing specially corresponding to them. They have no definite meaning, and are applied to a great variety of things of most different natures. In political economy, as in other sciences, it is absolutely essential to avoid using words of vague and varying meaning. If we were to write a treatise on gas, and to call all gases vapour instead of using their real names, the treatise would be absurd and incomprehensible.

Thus 'money' may mean gold, silver, copper, coin, Government notes, the notes of private banks, free notes, superintended notes, cheques, drafts, Consols, bonds, shares, wealth, riches, capital, credit, etc.

'Currency' may mean good gold coin or the most depreciated private note, Government bills or postage-stamps, international credit or I.O.U.'s.

Things so widely different cannot be treated under one head, and we contend that whichever is spoken of should be mentioned by its name. A collective name for many things may sometimes be convenient, but the words 'money' and 'currency' are so intimately and specially associated with things of opposite nature that they cannot be used without mental confusion. If their use could be discontinued in all economical and financial discussions, political economy, and even theories of banking, would cease to be a puzzle to many sensible people.

Most writers on banking have called coin money or currency, and then laboriously attempted to find or create theories which would hold good not only for coin, but for many other special meanings of these general terms. They seem to apprehend nothing but the coin which they call money. To many of them 'banking' is only dealing, warehousing, and lending money; 'interest' is the price and value of money; 'want of capital' is dearth of money, etc. Their explanation of the different stages of the development of banking is therefore more in harmony with the ideas of the people who at various periods initiated them, than with real economical facts.

When coin came into general use another considerable extension was given to co-operation. Exchanges were rendered easy under the form of buying and selling. A few men began to occupy themselves entirely with assisting the public in exchanges, and became merchants and shopkeepers.

From the first coin had two functions, that of an article of exchange, and that of a measurer of value. The latter is, and probably ever was, the more important, as only the smaller purchases and transactions were, as they are now, made with coin. Direct exchange of goods for goods did not cease because coin had come into use. Large transactions were carried on in this way still, the only difference being that the goods exchanged were '*valued*' in coin. Wholesale business is carried on in this way yet between wholesale firms, England and her Colonies, and between merchants of different countries.

But before the wholesale exchange of goods could be largely developed, a new medium of exchange had to be introduced, and this was '*credit.*' Buyers and sellers could not always meet each other, nor bring their goods simultaneously, especially when living far apart ; and it was both dangerous and expensive to send a messenger with coin each time goods were wanted. It was obviously convenient to send the goods upon trust until returns of other goods were made, and then to pay the difference in coin. Then it was found that the balance could be kept and booked from one transaction to another, and thus credit and book-keeping came into existence.

From these innovations the great advantage at once resulted that large transactions could be carried on with little or no coin, and yet calculated with as great a nicety as though effected with coin ; or, in other words, co-operation became much more easy, not only between neighbours, but between all civilized people all over the world. It will be perfectly clear that co-operation could not have largely developed without credit and with coin as the only medium of exchange, when the following evident economic truth is thoroughly grasped :

Gold, silver, or coin imported into a normal market to be used as a medium of exchange will not remain, but will leave that market again if all else remains unchanged.

If we suppose a market so situated that extra coin imported to be used as a medium of exchange could not leave, what would happen ? The coin would go down in value in exact proportion to the imported quantity, and being the measurer of value, this sinking of the value of coin would manifest itself in a rise of the price of goods in general. Consequently, if the quantity of coin were doubled the price of goods would be doubled, and the larger quantity of coin would facilitate the exchange of exactly as much produce as the smaller, and not more. In reality, no market can be found from which coin cannot be exported. When extra coin is forcibly introduced into a market, a fall in its value, or, which is the same, a general rise in the price of goods first follows, but this soon causes influx of goods from abroad and re-export of the imported gold.

The impossibility of increasing the circulating coin permanently by importing it is a most important fact generally overlooked by people who theorize on banking, and always by those who make bank laws. Were it but better appreciated, we should hear less about loans from England to improve the position of the ryots in India and fellahs in Egypt, etc., as such loans will simply raise the cost of production for these poor people, without procuring any higher price for their goods produced for export. Such loans always have and always will ruin those countries which receive them.

The very limited use coin can be put to, and the fact that no market can hold more than is natural to it, which, compared with the business transacted, is a very small quantity, proves the immense importance of credit.

When once introduced, credit was soon applied to all kinds of exchanges, even such as were originally effected with coin. The buyers, though solvent, could not always command the necessary amount of coin to pay cash for their purchases; they obtained credit from the seller and deferred the payment of the coin. Such credit was a great advantage to the purchaser, who thereby increased his working capital. But it was a sacrifice on the part of the seller, and also a risk. For this he recouped himself by charging interest or a higher price for the goods as compensation for the loan of his capital.

As the advantages of increasing capital by goods obtained on credit and by loans were great enough to admit of charging a high interest, *loans of capital* in the shape of coin were resorted to.

The seller could not always give the buyer the credit he required, not knowing him, or not being able to spare the capital. If the buyer had ever so good a reputation for solvency, but was short of coin, he could generally find no other way to complete his transaction than by borrowing the requisite capital in the shape of coin from some one who had a sufficiency. This service could not be expected without compensation, and interest was paid upon the borrowed capital. Lending coin against interest, or interest and commission, became a trade, and initiated banking.

The first bankers probably only lent their own coin; but gradually they began to receive such unemployed capital in the shape of coin as others did not wish to keep by them. The coin-lender or banker lent this capital to others, charging them a higher interest than he himself paid. This was the first stage of the development of banking.

Thus primitive banking took the form of coin-lending, and whilst apparently extending the use of coin it actually laid the foundation of a new medium of co-operation, which, whilst retaining the coin as measurer of value, was to supersede it as a medium of exchange to a very great extent—in London, for example, of about 98 per cent. in all wholesale transactions. Nevertheless, the opinion has unfortunately prevailed that banking is '*dealing in coin,*' or, to use the vague popular expression, '*money.*'

Dealing in coin is not the true function of banking, but is simply *one* of the means it uses to fulfil the all-important part it takes in the great division of labour which we call civilization. To prove this, it is only necessary to briefly summarise the preceding sketch of the development of banking.

We have seen that *co-operation* was the first source of wealth, and that in our modern society it is so more than ever, and to such an extent that wealth and co-operation are, economically speaking, almost synonymous. *Exchange of products* was the only possible way in which co-operation could be carried on under a system of individual freedom. As direct exchanges were necessarily limited, indirect exchanges became the next step forward in the development of co-operation. *Coin* was invented, but its use as a medium of exchange being strictly limited in consequence of its being the value measurer, *credit* became necessary. Direct credit met with the same insurmountable difficulties as direct exchanges, and *indirect credit* became indispensable for the further development of co-operation, and indirect credit could not be carried on without banking.

Banking, consequently, is the chief mechanism of *co-operation,* the indispensable medium of exchange for all the great business in a civilized country, a final squarer of accounts, and an institution which enables all to take part in the general co-operation of the world, keeping account of their contributions, and securing to them a share in the products.

If it is clear that credit cannot develop without a banking system, nor exchange without credit, nor division of labour without exchange, then obviously the function of banking is to facilitate co-operation, and coin-lending is only one of the means it uses for that great purpose.

We can easily conceive a banking system without coin or currency lending, nay, without coin altogether. Suppose our economic development had taken another direction, and that a community existed without coin. A central office for the squaring of the co-operation, with a due respect for private property, might be established in the following way : Cheque-books could be given to each person in proportion to his means. For each exchange or purchase the buyer could give a cheque to the seller for the amount of gold, or whatever be the value measurer of the country, agreed to as the price. The seller could transfer the cheque to some one else, in paying for his own purchase, endorsing it either to order or bearer ; or he could take it to the central office and have it put to his credit, and make his payment by drawing a cheque on the central office.

All transactions could thus be carried on by debiting the buyers and crediting the sellers. This system has actually been put into practice by banks. The *Mark Banco* of Hamburgh was never coined, and was nevertheless, or rather in consequence thereof, the safe value measurer for centuries throughout North-Eastern Europe. Hereafter we shall see that from force of circumstances our own banking has developed in this direction, and that the London Clearing House is not far different from such a central office of co-operation as we have here described.

The foregoing explanation will enable us to assume as axioms :

First. That banking was forced into existence as the indispensable medium of extending co-operation co-existent with the right of property and individual liberty.

Secondly. That the function of true banking is not to deal in and warehouse coin, but to facilitate co-operation in production and distribution.

Thirdly. That a banking system is good when it supplies mediums of exchange equal to the demand of all economically sound business, with the smallest possible increase in the use of the value measurer as medium of exchange.

II.

THE DEVELOPMENT OF BANKING IN ENGLAND.

THE preceding exposition of the nature and object of banking will, we trust, make quite intelligible the following short summary of the different stages of the development of banking in England, and assist us in forming an idea of the disastrous effects of the Bank Act of 1844.

The first general precursors of bank-notes, viz., bank drafts, were a considerable step forward. They were invented to avoid the necessity of carrying large quantities of coin—an inconvenient and dangerous practice.

The facility with which these drafts circulated, and their convenience in squaring a number of exchanges, greatly promoted their use. But in England the bank-note originated with the receipts of the goldsmiths of London for coin deposited. The holders of the receipts, when they wanted to dispose of the deposited amounts, found it convenient to transfer the receipt instead of drawing the coin, and large amounts of coin would therefore have remained for long periods in the strong-boxes of the goldsmiths, had they not discovered it to be both safe and profitable to lend them to others.

When the goldsmiths found that their receipts or notes circulated readily, and came for payment in quantities, and at intervals fairly regular and calculable, they began to lend fictitious receipts payable to bearer along with the coin, and increased thereby their profits.

There was no law to restrict their business in any way. It was to their own advantage to be prudent and honest. Some failures seem to have taken place among the goldsmiths, but they could not have been frequent or very disastrous, as they did not affect the credit of that body in general.

These primitive bankers seem to have been popular and generally sought by the business-men of London, to whom they were very helpful.

Their real economic importance was, however, not understood. They seemed only useful as dealers in coin, whilst, in fact, the new and improved medium they offered for exchanges caused business to develop rapidly, and to this

increased co-operation the goldsmith became indispensable.
All the business which passed through their books would
have had to cease if they had been repressed without being
replaced, because it would have been impossible to work it
with coin. The large quantity of coin would have raised
prices too much.

If the goldsmiths did not wittingly exercise prudence and
moderation in the issue of their notes, their business soon
compelled them to cultivate these virtues. When they
found their notes return in quicker ratio than they issued
them, they had to stop or curtail the issue, or all their coin
would have been cleared out, which would have meant to
them the loss of their credit, honour, and position, and
rendered any further banking business impossible.

The economic explanation of the demand for the goldsmiths' notes and bank-notes in general is this : The notes,
though requiring no more financial experience or education
in the handling than coin, and being used by the public as
such, were in reality nothing more than a medium for the
direct exchange of products and services, just as a great
general ledger might have been. They circulated in proportion to the business, and did not send up prices as a
corresponding imported quantity of gold would have done.

As circulating notes were being used as coin, the public
soon recognised them as such, and called them 'paper-
money.' The business of circulating notes was therefore
considered equivalent to money coining.

Now the function of coining had been regarded from
olden times as a princely privilege all over Europe, for no
other reason than that princes claimed it as such. The
same opinion prevails yet, but without any other reason
than the convenience of such an arrangement. History
furnishes many reasons why kings and Governments should
not have anything to do with coining, for they have fear-
fully abused and mismanaged it. Base coinage was for the
rulers a source of revenue, but for their subjects a source
of much trouble. The base coinage of the German Princes
was carried to such an extent that it was found expedient
not to coin the mark-banco of Hamburg at all, in order to
avoid its deterioration.

It is, however, of little moment who presides at the coining ; we merely wish to point out that coining being considered a royal privilege, it seemed natural that Government
should interfere with what was looked upon as paper-
coinage, and therefore it usurped the rights of the gold-

smiths. To this shallow view of things, coupled with the desire of the Government for a convenient means of raising capital, the world owes most of the State banks, and we our Bank Act.

Prejudice had its full swing. There was no knowledge of political economy to suggest any objection. A natural commercial liberty, which had not been misused, was suppressed quite unnecessarily, and only to gratify the prejudice against free note-issuing.

The greater number of note-issuing State banks have, like the Bank of England, their issue determined on a most extraordinary principle. The debt of the State to the bank, either by direct loan, or through the bank holding Government bonds, was, and still is, in many cases, at once the basis, regulator of, and security for, the notes. It is surprising that such a system should have been adopted at a time when notes were looked upon as 'money.'

This principle, had it been possible to carry it out to the full, would have been very convenient for prodigal Governments. According to it, the more the nation incurred debt the more it enriched itself; the more money it spent the more it had left. When put to a severe test it has led to depreciation of the notes, and suspension of gold payment.

It matters very little what kind of security is held for State notes, it is the clumsy interference of Government with banking at all which constitutes the great evil.

We have pointed out this absurdity only to show the total absence of principle and common sense in the most important of our economic laws.

The establishing of the Bank of England, and the grant of the privileges, the most important of which still exist, to the Bank, would in our day be styled a gigantic *job*. The King or the Government wanted gold, and to obtain it the people were deprived of a most precious liberty—viz., the right to carry on co-operation in the only effective way practicable under existing circumstances. The only excuse for the Government is that it did not realize what it was doing.

The amount of the loan which the Crown received as the price of the Bank monopoly was small to begin with ; but through successive Bank charters and new advances the debt of the State to the Bank has now reached about £14,000,000.

This is a very small sum compared either with the National Debt as a whole, or with the sum the English people yearly lose in the gigantic obstruction to trade caused by the absence of rational banking, as we shall explain further on. The history of banking in England from the first Bank Act up to the year 1844 is the history of the State Bank itself.

It is narrated in many ways in various books, but to one who reads it in the light of true political economy it illustrates almost on every page the absurdity of State interference with the banking of the people. This long period, though full of incident, shows no real steps in advance toward rational banking in England, the stagnation being a natural consequence of State interference.

The Bank Act of 1844 was indeed founded on some new theories; but these were of the most superficial and futile kind, and out of harmony with sound economy. Consequently, three years after it was passed it brought about precisely the state of things it was intended to prevent—namely, over-issue and scarcity of gold. As all this has been well described in several works (especially in Mr. Herbert Spencer's able but too fragmentary paper on 'State Interference in Banking'), and as we have but little space, we must refer the reader to these works for incidents. But it will be instructive to consider the economic position of the people under the Bank monopoly. During the long period from the establishment of the Bank of England to 1844, millions of Englishmen had a very hard struggle to improve their position, whilst, for the majority of the people, it was a constant problem how to live at all. It could not be otherwise. Co-operation through exchange had long before become the leading feature of the economic development of the country, especially in the towns. Exchange of products and services was a necessity, not only to prosperity, but to livelihood.

The great majority of the people having neither capital, coin, nor credit, and depending for their living entirely upon the exchange of their services against products, suffered exceedingly when the action of the Government threw successive obstacles in the way of co-operation and of exchange. One of the worst, though the least understood, of these obstacles was the Bank Act, curtailing and corrupting as it did the only possible medium of co-operation, namely, banking. *Coin*, of which the market in its miserable state could not hold much, and the ruinous *direct credit*, or money-lending, were the only means left to carry on the division of labour. The result was that work was scarce and under-paid, that enterprise or business was extremely hampered, and proved risky and productive of indebtedness.

At first, and especially in the country, the people did not fully feel the effect of this limitation of exchange and consequent obstruction to co-operation, because the direct co-operation—that is, co-operation without exchange—and compulsory division of labour was carried on by the feudal mediums of co-operation, viz., the *masters*. Work was exchanged directly against products. Food and clothing being derived from the ground, the landowners in the country exercised the same economic functions as the banks in the towns. They provided the work, often using compulsion, and distributed the products, that is, they distributed as little as possible, and kept for themselves as much as they could.

But gradually, as the population increased and competition became more keen, the evil influence of the unsound economic system of the nation began to affect the landowners, especially through the loans they contracted. They found it more advantageous to let the land at a high rent than to personally conduct its cultivation; in few words, our modern economic system was developed. Its characteristics are supposed to be individual initiative and freedom of action. According to this, supply and demand should be the only regulators of division of labour, *i.e.*, give every man his work and his share in the product.

There are obviously only two directions in which the economic development of a nation can progress, either towards entire State regulation of all labour or towards entire freedom in the division of labour—that is, a free and natural balance between demand and supply. The English people have wisely chosen the latter direction, though in it they progress very slowly.

During the centuries through which England has progressed from feudalism to free division of labour, the people have suffered terribly, because they have been losing the mediums of co-operation which feudalism supplied, whilst the essential parts of the mechanism of free division of labour have been obstructed by foolish legislation. Most unreasonable monopolies and most foolish prohibitions existed to an incredible extent. The most pernicious of these, after the Bank Monopoly, were perhaps the protective duties. Protection obstructed the co-operation of our nation with other nations, as the Bank Law obstructed the co-operation between man and man, between labour and capital, between workers and thinkers, etc. Protection openly prevented the exchange and supply of food while the people were starving, whereas the way in which the Bank Law worked its evil effects was hidden from the people. The smaller evil, the Corn Laws, was therefore abolished; and the larger one, Bank Monopoly, yet *remains to be abolished.*

The blind and illogical struggle of the people for easier co-operation had no chance against monopoly. From lack of economic knowledge the right direction to progress in banking was not found. But at last a great step in advance was taken, and co-operation developed enormously. This step was not the result of any action on the part of Government, nor of the oppressed business men of England. No; it is an astounding fact that the grandest development of English banking, the first condition for the great modern extension of England's business, wealth, and power, was due entirely to the happy discovery in the year 1833 of a flaw in the Bank Act!

In spite of the careful wording of the Act, the object of which was to monopolise practically all joint-stock banking in London, it was found legal to carry on joint-stock banking by companies composed of more than six partners, so long as note-issuing did not form part of the business. The directors of the Bank of England of course protested, but commonsense prevailed. Minor legal difficulties were, however, raised, with the result that only one joint-stock bank was formed up to 1844, viz., the London and Westminster Bank. But the Bank Charter of that year sanctioned the new interpretation of the Bank Act, and prevented chicanerie.

Then began the establishing of large non-issuing banking companies in London, which not only enabled the people to reap greater advantages from accomplished improvements in other directions, but gave also a grand, direct impulse to all business. The great obstruction to business was now less intense, and the prosperity which resulted was great.

Since 1844 the export and import of Great Britain alone has increased from £110,000,000 to £700,000,000. It is as impossible as it is also useless to try to determine how much of this increase is due to Free Trade and other causes, many of them great and powerful, and how much to this extension of banking; but every business man can understand that such an amount of business as we now put through would be perfectly impossible without the present banking accommodation.

The patience of the English people under this Bank Act would seem very strange if the history of banking and the popular prejudices respecting coin and banking did not account for it. Though the English have made the Bank Act themselves, they seem to regard it as a law of nature, and in spite of its defect, they dare not mend it.

It is found so meritricious that a temporary suspension of it is sometimes proved necessary and the only means of escape from national financial ruin, and yet it is not abolished! When once the impending calamity is averted, the old cause of it is speedily reinforced. Then it is found that a small loophole in the shape of a flaw in the Bank Act, which enables the people to lessen its oppressiveness a little, produces the most remarkable financial development the country ever experienced; and yet the bad law is upheld—no inquiry into its working is suggested in Parliament, though it seems natural the people should try to find, or invent, some more of these happy flaws.

The new feature slowly introduced by the non-issuing private bankers and made general through the large banking companies was the cheque system. With the large new banks, banking accounts and cheques became most important mediums of co-operation.

Both cheques and banking accounts were originally introduced, and the system afterwards extended, with the same narrow object as all other improvements in banking, viz., to facilitate coin-lending; but regarded from an economic point of view, they fulfilled the object of real banking much better than coin-lending could possibly do.

Though both banking accounts and cheques were actually promises to pay coin, they circulated capital in all possible forms, measured in coin, in the most easy and simple way, with the assistance of very little cash. In the bank-books one customer was debited whilst another was credited, without any payment of the actual value measurer, coin. Cheques squared accounts just as coin, whilst in reality they were, as bank-notes are, only mediums to keep account of contributions towards the general co-operation and distribution of products. Instead of writing the amount due to the bearer to the credit of a banking account, it was credited to the bearer on this portable account, the cheque.

The next great step in advance took place when the use-

fulness of the cheques and banking accounts was extended
through the establishment of the London Clearing House.
This, again, was the outcome of a blind groping for means
to simplify coin-lending, and save labour in the bank
offices.

But from the economic point of view it fulfils, within the
narrow scope which the Bank Act allows, in a perfect way
the most important function in the general division of
labour. It affords the easiest, and simplest, and cheapest
way of exchanging all kinds of capital and services, exactly
measured in coin, without the use of coin.

But unfortunately this valuable piece of mechanism, the
crowning wheel in the machinery of co-operation, relieves,
owing to the Bank Act, only a very small part of the great
demand for extended division of labour; and the most
important parts, the preparatory wheels or local banks of
a rational character, are wanting all over the Empire.

That such is the effect of the Bank Act of 1844 we hope
to make clear in the following chapters.

III.

ON SOME GENERALLY RECOGNISED EVIL CONSEQUENCES OF THE BANK ACT OF 1844.

THE monopoly of the Bank of England, and the centralization which it naturally implies, produce many evil consequences, and of these we shall now treat.

They may be divided into two classes—viz., those *generally recognised*, and those *not generally recognised*. The
former require, of course, but little explanation ; the latter,
and incomparably the most important, we must treat more
exhaustively, because they have not been explained before,
and because, being the key to the solution of a great
number of difficult economic enigmas of our times, the importance of their effect, and the obscure nature of their
influence, alike demand a full explanation.

In this short chapter we have only to do with the
generally recognised evil consequences of the Bank Act of
1844.

By the following provisions this Act gave the Bank of
England an effective monopoly of note-issuing :

1st. 'That no bank which issued notes before 1844 bo allowed to extend its issue.'

2nd. ' That no other bank be allowed to issue notes at all.' With the growing business of England, the permission to some few banks to keep a limited amount of notes in circulation cannot take away from the Bank Charter its character of a monopoly. Moreover, the Bank of England is, by another provision, entitled to take up two-thirds of the issue of any bank which may forego its right of issuing notes.

The Bank of England itself is allowed to issue fourteen million pounds of notes (plus the above-mentioned 'two-thirds of the issue renounced by the private banks), against the debt of the State to the Bank of a corresponding amount.

Besides this the Bank may issue notes up to any amount for which it has in its possession equivalent value in precious metals.

These privileges, which monopolize a most valuable public right, evidently do not confer very great advantages on the Bank of England. If the Bank Act were suspended for ever the Bank of England would, in spite of competition, profit enormously by it; and most of the directors are probably well aware that their monopoly of issue is nothing but a white elephant.

The Bank of England, like all note-issuing banks, must look closely after its metallic cash. When the stock of gold goes down the Bank must of course lessen and avoid increasing liabilities payable on demand, especially in the form of notes ; it must lend and discount a reduced amount. Instead of declining some bills and securities, and only taking others, the Bank reduces its payments by raising the rate of discount all round, which seems fairer, and is decidedly more profitable to the Bank. A high rate of interest naturally debars a great amount of business ; and when a large number of transactions are made impossible, a less amount of notes is demanded and issued. The Bank having thus reduced its issue of notes, there is a better demand for those in circulation, and they do not come back to be exchanged for gold in the same proportion as before. Fewer notes coming back, less coin being paid out, and the regular influx of gold remaining as before, the reserve of gold soon increases.

This is how the raising of the rate of discount increases the gold reserve.

2

But there is another theory, at first sight apparently less unpalatable, in that it does not give prominence to the coincident curtailment of business; it is that the raising of the rate of discount causes gold to leave foreign markets, where the rate is lower, and to come into the vaults of the Bank.

Now many business-men in England know through experience that wherever the gold may come from, the process by which it gets into the vaults of the Bank is exactly such as we have described it.

The theory just mentioned seems to presuppose that foreign capitalists keep their capital in bar-gold or English sovereigns; that capital can be withdrawn from foreign places in sufficient amount to reduce the rate in London without raising it abroad; that gold can be shipped from one market to another without causing a variation in the rate of exchange which would force it back again—all which never could happen. It also seems to imply either that the Bank of England pays interest on deposits, or that very large amounts of gold are coined when the rate of discount is high. That the latter is not the case is proved by the fact that the coinage has not been large in the years in which the Bank-rate has been high. Of the years from 1840 to 1883 the coinage was highest in 1872, amounting to over £15,000,000, but the average rate was 4⅜ per cent. In 1863 the average rate reached 7½ per cent., while the coinage was only about nine and a half millions.

The theory of a high rate of discount attracting gold from abroad must therefore be regarded as a figure of speech. It may have the effect of lowering the rates of exchange, which would be the necessary preliminary phenomenon before foreign gold would come here to be melted or pawned; but such a lowering of the foreign exchange would be the result of sales of goods abroad in exceptional quantities—a consequence of a general fall in prices caused by the curtailed business in England which must follow the raising of the Bank-rate.

In virtue of its privileges, but by no means in virtue of the importance of its business, the Bank of England is the centre of finance, not only for Great Britain, but for the whole empire. This centralization system extends the direct influence of the Bank over a very large amount of business, and a still larger amount is influenced indirectly. The discount-rate (as being an index of the general policy of the Bank), is the standard and guide of a great number of business establishments. Consequently, when the rate is raised by the Bank of England, it causes, even apart from the reduced quantity of notes and gold in circulation, a general curtailing of business; a general disinclination to discount or lend; a general tendency to withhold credit. Each advance of the rate of discount of the Bank of England causes, therefore, great trouble to all who are not discounters, severe losses to many, and ruin to some.

To create a panic instead of only a disturbance is merely a question of the figure of the advance. By suddenly raising the rate very high the Bank could produce a fearful catastrophe.

The evil consequences generally complained of as resulting from this system are:

1st. That too much power is given to the Directors of the Bank of England, and that they have not the liberty to use their power judiciously, but have often no other choice than to disturb the whole commerce of the empire or cause the Bank to stop payment.

2nd. That disturbances are caused artificially when the state of trade is perfectly healthy.

3rd. That the evil done is not compensated by the end obtained—viz., replenishing the gold reserve of one single bank.

4th. That causes quite foreign to English business, and even to business in general, may create a demand for gold from the Bank, and induce it to advance its rate of discount, thereby producing all the evils which generally follow such a measure.

5th. That the supply of credit (a medium of exchange which in our days clears 99 per cent. of all business passing through the banks of London, while coin only clears 1 per cent.) is dependent on one small gold reserve belonging to one bank.

6th. That one or more rich men can, by drawing a certain amount of gold simultaneously from one bank, manipulate prices at their option, and even throw all business into confusion.

7th. That the fact of the whole financial system of the country being made amenable to what may be described as a convenient handle for mischief, and such an enormous amount of promises to pay based on one single gold reserve, easily manipulated or secured, places the country, in case of war with a European Power or a political disturbance at home, in extreme danger.

2—2

8th. That through the limited supply of notes financial depressions develop into panics.

9th. That the Bank Act, while exposing commerce and prosperity to all kinds of losses and dangers, has never been found useful except when suspended.

These objections to the Bank Act are general among business men who have given the subject any attention, and although not using the exact wording in which one usually hears and reads the complaints, we have tried to give an exact expression to the general opinion on the subject.

The objections are important enough to invite an inquiry, and the objectors are numerous and influential enough to bring about a reform if they would only cease recommending remedies worse than the disease, and drop their unreasonable prejudices against rational banking. No sensible Government would meddle with such an important matter by doing patchwork in the wrong direction for the sake of doing something; and what Government in England could legislate in the teeth of a strong prejudice which possesses almost every mind?

IV.

EXCESSIVE USE OF THE VALUE MEASURER AS A MEDIUM OF EXCHANGE, AND THE EVIL CONSEQUENCES THEREOF.

THE two leading features of the Bank Act of 1844 are (1) the State supervision over the notes, and (2) the monopoly of issue.

The State supervision over the Bank of England's notes makes them practically as safe as coin, and they circulate consequently all over the country with the same facility as coin. Their effect on their market, which is the whole country, is therefore exactly the same as that of coin. The notes are handled by the people, the banks, and, what is more important, by the Bank of England itself, as coin; and in issuing them the Bank need use none of the nice considerations which under a free system, such as the Scotch banking was before 1844, become paramount. The notes of the Bank of England are therefore paper coin, and their issue is, as far as the effect on the market is concerned, equivalent to production or importation of so much gold.

The fact that the Bank does not issue any notes which are not coin has strongly influenced, and does yet influence, the business of the Bank, tending to give it the character of coin-lending, as is indeed the case with most State banks. Now we have seen in our first chapter that money-lending against pawned securities is not fully developed rational banking, but simply the first step of primitive banking, and one of the ways in which banking strives to fulfil its mission, namely, to work the exchanges. Whether the stereotyping of the Bank of England in this primitive form has impelled and confirmed the business of the private banks in the same direction, and thus explains to some extent the great difference we find between English and French banking methods, would be an interesting inquiry, but out of place here. We have only to deal with the fact that our private banks work their business in the same way as the Bank of England, and that it consists chiefly in lending their own capital, the deposits of coin they attract, and the credit they can create, to those who present the best securities. A kind of business which requires large capital, large credit, and large turn-over to pay at all, except, of course, when it is worked as usury or pawnbroking.

The other leading feature of the Act of 1844, namely, the monopoly of note issue, which prevents the existence of issuing banks of a rational kind (the fourteen issuing banks we have are more deposit banks than issuing banks), tends more powerfully and more directly to make small local banks unprofitable when not worked on usurious principle. The result of the two leading features of our banking system is that we have no banks in poor districts, however capable they may be of economic development; nor in thinly populated districts, however rich they may be in raw materials; nor in thickly populated places, where work is in great demand but capital scarce and inert; nor amongst small people beginning trades—amongst, so to say, the roots of production.

Where there is no banking the co-operation must be worked with coin. That in England an excessive use of coin is now unavoidable becomes evident when we consider the following facts:

It does not pay a bank under the present system to open accounts with small firms. Most English banks demand from £50 to £100 deposit, and they do not like to see this deposit drawn out. In London there are only one or two banks which make it a business to open small accounts, and these are more savings than commercial banks. In a place in France of about 7,000 inhabitants, we found there three or four competing commercial bankers aiding large and small producers most effectively. How can a small producer or distributor afford to keep a balance of £100 or even £50 in a bank for the single advantage of facility in cashing his cheques? He has his capital invested in houses, furniture, machines, tools, raw material, goods in process of manufacture, and must also give some short credit to his customers.

Only those who are capitalists as well as producers and distributors can afford the luxury of a banking account, and therefore a very great number have none. They do their business with cash entirely. And do such as have a banking account, generally opened by the paying in actual cash, clear all their business through the bank, or even a large proportion of it? All the small, a majority of the medium, and many of the large holders of banking accounts, square the larger part of their business with cash. It is not the custom in this country, as in France, to draw and accept bills for all purchases in the home trade. Bills are used to some extent, but are not the rule. They are drawn exceptionally, and mostly to serve as a security for cash loans. Purchases of both raw material and manufactured goods are generally made for cash either on delivery or in a short time after. When paid for by cheques these are very frequently turned into cash at once.

The use of coin is greatly increased by the fact that in many small centres of trade there are, as we have mentioned, no banks at all. In such places the bulk of the transactions are, sooner or later, settled by cash. All business men who buy in small quantities, all who sell in small quantities, all who employ labour and pay wages, are compelled to use a great amount of coin, as no small notes exist. All the turn-over of the working-classes—all the wages they receive and all their purchases—is cleared by coin.

From what has been said, we trust it is clear, that in England the banking system compels the use of a very large quantity of cash in proportion to the business transacted. Owing to the absence of small bankers of the French style, working the co-operation with bills—to the absence of banks issuing small notes, and to the absence in many places even of banks and bank offices of the English type—a very great part of the English co-operation is entirely unassisted by banking, and has to depend exclusively on the supply of coin and coin notes—that is, notes for which a corresponding quantity of gold has been locked up in the bank or exported. This system necessitates large quantities of gold to work even a comparatively small business, and for any increase of our activity, especially in productive trades, we must augment the supply of gold considerably.

To understand the ruinous effect which the compulsory presence of such a comparatively large quantity of gold, and the constant attempts to import more, must have on the business of the people, we must fully realize the importance of the economic axiom mentioned in the first chapter, viz., that gold, like any other goods imported into a market in excess of the consumption—that is, increasing the stock—will leave that market again, or if artificially prevented from leaving, will fall in value in exact proportion to the quantity imported in excess. This is, or ought to be, a self-evident fact; it has been proved a thousand times, and is proved every day by facts and by statistics to those who take the trouble to read them aright.

But it seems that deductions from statistical figures un-accompanied by intelligent explanations have but little power to convince. This axiom is anyhow not believed in by the Parliaments of the Continent and of the United States. Their economy is founded on quite opposite premises. Besides, there exists a general opinion that gold, imported to be used as medium of exchange (coin), in such business as promises to become wealth-producing, will not lower the value of coin and leave, but will stay in the market. As it is necessary to disprove this fallacy, and as we shall have to deduce from the above-mentioned economic truth conclusions which will appear stupendous, we shall try to be as plain as possible, and to call in evidence such proofs as we can examine every day.

It is evident that the value of any kind of goods, or indeed of anything, is regulated by the proportion of demand to supply. When the demand for an article increases and the supply remains the same, this article goes up in price. When the supply increases and the demand remains the same, it goes down in price. All the markets of the civilized world illustrate this fact. Wherever there is an excess of one kind of goods, the low price causes shipment to some place where it will command a higher price. The difference in price pays for the transport, risk, and trouble.

We shall now show that gold is subject to exactly the

same economic laws. Let us suppose that a million pounds' worth of gold ingots are forcibly moved, say from Berlin to London. If the gold is not consumed for any special object apart from commerce, but thrown on the market in some shape, there is an alteration in the relative supply of gold in the two markets of £2,000,000, as there is £1,000,000 more in London and £1,000,000 less in Berlin ; but if the gold is destroyed, hoarded, or re-exported from England, the change in the relative supply is only £1,000,000. In either case the stock of gold ingots, or uncoined gold, is £1,000,000 less in Berlin. Suppose that the demand there remains the same, the holders of the remaining gold in ingots will be harder to make terms with. Such holders may be manufacturers requiring gold for their pro-ductions, dealers in precious metals who keep it in stock, banks who keep it as a reserve, the Royal Mint, which is bound to supply coin to the Government, etc. Gold would therefore be less freely offered to or by these parties.

The first effect would be to raise the price of gold in ingots sufficiently to cover the small difference between ingots and coin which might exist as a coinage fee. Gold ingots and coin would then be equal in value, and gold-smiths, and other consumers of gold, would melt coin, which would thus become scarcer. The banks, or the State Bank, would consequently have to meet a heavier demand for gold coin, and would have to take measures to increase their stock. This they could do only by importing gold from abroad. If they took such action they would pro-bably import it from England (the market where most of the new gold from the gold-producing countries is landed), paying for it in the usual course by drafts on London.

There would thus be an increased demand in Berlin for drafts on London, and the rate of exchange would certainly go up—that is, the pound sterling would be quoted higher on the Berlin Bourse. The effect of the pound sterling fetching a higher price than German notes, and even than German gold, is that German products sold to England obtain a higher price than when sold in Germany, though the nominal price quoted in gold be the same.

This is equal to a premium on the export of German goods to England, and thither an additional quantity of German goods would consequently go in preference to seek-ing home consumption, which, besides, would be already curtailed by the scarcity of gold. This extra export of goods pays the drafts remitted against the gold ordered from London, which thus would come back to Berlin from where we supposed it removed.

We see from this that forcible export of gold from a market raises the price of gold in that market, both as compared with foreign gold and with goods in general.

Also, that transactions intended to be actual transfers of gold from one market to another resolve themselves (through the incapacity of markets to hold more or less coin than is natural to them) into transfers of goods other than coin.

We shall now see how the supposed forcible removal of gold to London would affect the English market.

The gold would either be thrown on the market or kept out of it. The latter case could happen only under unusual circumstances, such as immediate consumption for a special abnormal purpose, secret hoarding, or re-exportation. In such cases it would have no direct effect on the market. All the effect would be indirect—namely, cheapening of German goods, as we have already seen, consequently lessened export to Germany, increased import of German goods, and a corresponding stagnation in the production in England.

If, on the other hand, the imported gold were thrown on the market, it would increase the quantity of coin. Whether it were put through the Mint, added to the Bank reserve to increase the issue of coin notes, or absorbed in manufactures, thereby taking the place of gold which else would have been withdrawn from circulation, would make no difference.

As the ultimate result is the same, let us suppose that the gold is coined. The new coin would, on issue, be invested in some manner, something would be actually bought by it either for consumption, storing, or manufacturing.

In any case goods of some kind are withdrawn from the market, stocks are reduced, and prices go up. That is equivalent to gold falling in value. The high prices, in face of the increased rapidly circulating stock of gold in the country, do not check the home consumption, but impede the export, which falls off; the consumption increases, partly for reproduction and partly as a result of larger profits, and is supplied by increased import; the diminished export and increased import are balanced by payment of the difference in gold, which thus leaves the country again, and the gold supply recovers its disturbed level.

It is then evident that the power of imported gold to

send up prices is, at least, twice as effective when the gold is used for coin or otherwise thrown on the market, as when it is withheld from circulation or hidden.

The supposed case of forcible removal of gold is one which seldom if ever happens in reality. Under normal circumstances removals of large quantities of gold, except the regular supply from the mines, are not frequent, and are generally made for abnormal purposes. As gold forcibly removed from one market to another always returns again to the market from which it came, the double journey is generally avoided by variations in the rate of exchange, and the final result, removal of goods, is arrived at directly.

When a large amount of capital, measured in gold and treated for as gold, is to be removed from one nation's market to that of another as a loan, tribute, indemnity, or from any other cause outside general commerce, it might at first be supposed that gold would be actually sent. But the transfer of the amount is usually accomplished in the following way : Drafts are drawn from the country where the capital is to be received on the country which has to pay. These drafts are sold in the home market, and as they are many and heavy they must be sold cheap. The rates of exchange therefore go down. This constitutes a premium on import of goods, and an obstacle to export in the receiving country. Import increases and export decreases, until the increase of the former and decrease of the latter (other things remaining normal) altogether correspond with the amount of the imported capital, which thus has been delivered in goods, though it was agreed to be paid in gold.

The fall in the price of the gold to be imported is anticipated before the gold can be shipped, and the prompt shipment of goods anticipates its return. Thanks to short-sighted Parliaments and prejudiced Ministers we have plenty of examples of such operations. The effect of imported gold, or rather, of gold intended for import, on prices and on the rates of exchange, causes large international transactions to result very differently from anticipation. Large war indemnities ultimately prove to the country which receives them, not a source of wealth, but a total upset of values in general, causing first a great falling off of the export, an enormous increase in consumption, and a crop of bad speculations ; and then, as a reaction, ruined production and commerce, and loss of capital. The 'Gründer Zeit,' or flush period in Germany, was soon followed by a crash from which that country suffered for many years, and which was worse for her than the payment of the indemnity was for France.

When the real value of gold indemnities is understood we shall have one less inducement to war.

The railway loans to many minor foreign countries furnish similar examples. Countries where land is of little cost, where iron and wood are plentiful, labour cheap, employment scarce, and provisions abundant, have not found any better way to construct a railway with their own material, and by their own work-people, than by borrowing *the whole amount* of the cost in foreign countries.

The result is that when the railway is made it costs twice or three times as much as it ought to have done, and the statistics of the years during which the loans have been drawn show that to make a railway in such countries demands the importation of astounding quantities of velvet, jewelry, perfumery, wines, sauces, toys, etc., besides a considerable quantity of such classes of goods as form, under normal circumstances, the staple production and export of the country.

All such follies result from overlooking the fact that an import of a quantity of gold must reduce proportionately the value of all the gold in the country, and that such import is naturally replaced by an import of goods. To deny this fact would be to deny that there ever is, was, or can be a variation of the rates of exchange.

As under the Bank Act of England the most important part of the co-operation can only be carried on with large quantities of coin or coin notes, we must come to the following conclusions :

That the presence of a large quantity of coin, which the Bank Act renders necessary to the transaction of business, defeats the object of business—viz., profit—by raising the cost of production here and lowering the price of sale abroad.

We are left the choice between two such desperate conditions as want of necessary mediums of exchange, or little or no profit on our trade. Each improvement in business must, under our normal circumstances, carry within itself the cause of its destruction, and bad times become the natural state. We deprive ourselves of the most necessary condition for profitable co-operation, namely, low cost of production, while we materially decrease the cost of production for our foreign competitors. We are obliged, under our normal circumstances, to struggle against the effect of the worst imaginable medium of co-operation by working hard, taking great risks, reducing or sacrificing our profits, and by paying such wages as are paid in the East of London now, or let our workmen starve.

All improvements and exertions to ameliorate our position, such as the invention of labour-saving machines, perfected division of labour, improved communications, increased capital, opening of new markets, etc., will produce only momentary relief. As soon as these improvements result in an increase in production or an increase in business, the additional coin required to carry it on will again reduce the profit.

Production being unprofitable, or tending to become so when extended, as a necessary arithmetical result of our using the value measurer as the chief medium of exchange, makes us think that we suffer from over-production, while 90 per cent. of humanity are short of every kind of comfort and luxury, and a large proportion have not even the simplest necessaries of life, all of which can be obtained only by an immense increase of production.

Similarly, because our system of finance makes work unprofitable, we are led to think that employment is naturally scarce, though employment alone can lessen the existing general misery, and our globe supplies inexhaustible stores of raw material.

Such are the consequences of the Bank Act under this head. They may be summarised thus : Capital and credit are made scarce and dear, while coin is made too cheap. The very contrary should of course be effected by a good banking system.

We have spoken of the effect of the Bank Act as being most severe under 'normal' conditions, and hinted that we are just now experiencing this state of things. We have done so because the periods of comparative prosperity which we have experienced since 1844, in spite of the Bank Act, must be considered abnormal.

These periods of prosperity were due to causes strong enough to counter-balance or hide the evil effects of the Bank Act.

We shall simply enumerate some of these causes, and briefly point out their effects.

1st. The establishment of Free Trade gave an immense impetus to business by lowering the cost of production, and enabling us to utilize and co-operate with foreign industry, thereby giving us a decided advantage in all the neutral markets.

2nd. The discovery of the flaw in the Bank Act removed a small part of its obstructiveness to business by permitting the establishment of the great joint-stock banks. This facilitated co-operation to such an extent that it has been possible to raise our turn-over enormously, unhampered by a corresponding increase in the quantity of the circulating value measurer.

3rd. The economic vagaries of other nations with respect to loans. The present amount of State debts, exclusive of the English, reaches the fearful sum of about £3,600,000,000. A very large part of this has been taken up in England since 1844, and every penny of it has been given not in coin, but in goods !

Those loans which have not been taken up in England have still given a great impetus to English industry, as each country taking a loan not only anticipates and consumes in a short time a part of its future earnings for centuries to come, but also prevents its own export of goods other than raw materials. England, borrowing but little, and not at all abroad, has had the greatest benefit from these mistakes.

But this cause of brisk trade will not occur again. The States either have no more credit, or they cannot pay any more interest, or they see the error of their ways. We have now to face the reaction, namely, a great many countries sending us their products as payment of interest without being able to afford any return in English goods. This should be a source of wealth and a blessing to England, but the Bank Act makes it a curse, and a source of misery for our working classes.

4th. Since 1844 the bulk of the great railway systems have been constructed. A great part of the capital and of the material has been supplied from England, and the consumption of such material as has not come from England has, however, caused prices all round to be high, and the demand good.

We shall have gradual extensions of railways, but never such enormous development again.

5th. Since 1844 we have seen navigation undergo a complete change. Wooden sailing ships have been replaced by iron steamers, mostly of English make, and what we have said concerning the railways applies to this change in shipping. It will not occur again.

6th. Exceptionally rich gold districts have been discovered and utilized. This has caused a rise in prices all over the world—a momentary prosperity, and large consumption. As soon as the ebb in prices began, this ephemeral prosperity came to an end.

7th. Since 1844 whole nations have been built up in America, Australia, New Zealand, etc., all with mostly English capital, that is, English manufactured goods. These countries will no doubt develop yet, especially if they adopt a less foolish economy; but such a stride as from a virgin state to high civilization will not again take place in so short a time. Whatever progress there may be, it will not have England for its base, as each country has now established a base of its own.

There were no doubt many more causes of prosperity between 1844 and 1884, but we have pointed out the most powerful.

The effect of all these impulses to business in England has been to increase our export and import from about £110,000,000 to £730,000,000, and it can be understood that under such circumstances there would be no grumbling against the Bank Act, especially as the prosperous period began almost simultaneously with the last Bank Charter. But the true economist might even during the most prosperous of these forty years have pointed out plenty of proofs that there was 'something rotten in the state' of Great Britain. While trade was at its best the condition of a very large proportion of working men, and still more of women, was very bad. In those parts of the empire where the abnormal causes of prosperity could not produce direct effects, as in Ireland and India, poverty has been growing steadily. The Irish population has decreased considerably, and so will the English if we do not now alter our method of co-operation. In India about 40 per cent. of the ryots are now paupers. All will be paupers shortly if we do not allow the people to carry on their division of labour by sensible means.

V.

LABOUR AND CAPITAL SEVERED.—USURY PROTECTED AT THE
EXPENSE OF LABOUR AND CAPITAL.

THE total capital of the banks and bankers of Great Britain,
together with the amount of deposits with them, the total
of the balances in their customers' favour, and the great
amount of capital circulated by the credit the banks create
—all this wealth represents a very large proportion of what
may be called the working capital of the nation ; and the
banks have, practically, the control of all this wealth. The
business of the country and its whole economy must, therefore, necessarily depend very much upon the manner in
which this trust is fulfilled.

The banks do not profess to employ the capital they hold
directly in production or distribution ; they simply discount
with it, or lend it—that is, they entrust it to other people.
It is, consequently, of great importance to whom this working capital of the nation is entrusted.

A bank could never be regarded as a charitable or
patriotic institution. It is a business, and the banker, like
any other business-man, must be actuated entirely by the
consideration of his own advantage—of course, within the
limits of honesty. The question, therefore, arises—Is the
interest of the banks, under the banking system resulting
from our Bank Act, identical with that of the nation ; or is
it indifferent, or even opposed to it ?

We can reply to this by finding out to whom the
banks give the preference in granting credits. Bound to
look after their own advantage, and generally charging the
same rate of interest and commission to all their customers,
English banks, in granting credits, are as a rule guided by
the securities offered. They give preference to the borrower
who presents the best and most convenient pledges for the
credit, be it his own name, several names, or some kind of
capital deposited or lodged.

As we in England are but little acquainted with other
banking systems than our own, it will be useful to point out
here that there are banking systems where the bankers are
not guided, in discounting, exclusively by the securities.
We shall mention two systems under which the banker

has a natural interest in being guided, not by the security, but by the nature of the business which is offered. These we may call the French and the old Scotch systems. By the latter we mean Scotch banking previous to 1844.

The average French banker of the class so generally and so numerously scattered over France, is interested in discounting as exclusively as possible for such producers or distributors as make it their business to send the products of the place, neighbourhood, or local markets away to other markets, and who do so with a profit to themselves.

The reason of this is very simple. The chief business of the banker consists in discounting bills. All bills drawn on other places he can, with his own endorsement, send away to other bankers, generally in some large centre, such as Paris. For these remittances he obtains, in return, bills drawn on his own market, and he thus increases his daily cash receipts, and can extend his operations. If he does not receive the full amount of paper in return, he can generally draw his own drafts on Paris for the difference, which suits him equally well. On the other hand, if he discounts promissory notes, or bills drawn from and payable in his own place, he cannot use them in the same way. He must keep them *en portefeuille* until maturity, and is thereby deprived of the use of his capital for a long time. By taking such paper he would accomplish only a very small yearly turn-over ; while, when taking only the first-mentioned kind, his turn-over is limited only to the extent of his connection and the business of the place.

His interest is, then, identical with the economic development of the country, as his advantage is to hold credit at the disposal of wealth-producing and work-giving people, or those who send away profitably produced goods, and to withhold it from the consumers and speculators, and those engaged in losing or unprofitable concerns, in so far as they attract and consume capital.

That a bank under the old Scotch system would be in exactly the same position we shall show further on.

In France there are financial institutions which lend capital against security of land, buildings, goods, funds and shares, etc. ; but they do not form a part of the great net-work of bankers who work the co-operation of the country. The existence of this latter kind of bankers is due to a slow and gradual development, and to traditions peculiar to France and some other countries, but which we have not experienced. As, then, the French banking system cannot exist in England, and as the far better one, the old Scotch system, is prohibited by law, all English banks are working somewhat after the style of the exceptional financial institutions of France, to which we have referred as lending against pledges. The business of our banks consists chiefly in receiving deposits of capital from those who have it to spare, and lending it to those who can use it and pay for its use, and in creating credit in favour of those whom they deem can be trusted, irrespective of the use to which it is put. The English banks have, therefore, no such special interest in common with that of the country as the French bankers have, and as the Scotch banks had, their chief duty and advantage being to look out for good and convenient securities.

The consequence is that the bulk of the working capital of the country is held in preference at the disposal of firms or individuals who are rich or supposed to be rich, who dispose of large quantities of goods, shares, or similar securities, who enjoy already a large credit, who do a *large* business, whether useful or hurtful, profitable or losing. In these classes of men and firms we find all those who borrow to consume, who speculate in the funds and shares, goods, land and house property, who corner markets, deal in limited liability companies, give large credits to consumers or to foreign commerce, who import largely, who over-trade, over-build, and all those who do a losing or spurious business, to the great injury of honest commerce, with the sole object of keeping afloat and being in a position to discount. If we could inquire into all the advances and loans granted by English banks on funds, shares, land, property, dock-warrants, bills of lading, promissory notes, personal guarantee and accommodation bills, the smaller part would be found to have any direct connection with healthy production.

The banks cannot be blamed for this. The law compels them to be money-lenders, and money-lenders they are.

While the banks thus gather up the working capital of the country, and hand it over in great part to the non-productive businesses, they divert that capital from the wealth-producing and work-giving trades; and this is a great evil.

We know that any nation which does not live on foreign loans cannot consume more than they produce; and that consequently not only the export trade, but also the import trade, depends entirely on the production, which, therefore,

3

is our only source of wealth, except the interest on money invested abroad.

If, therefore, the working capital of the country is for the greater part disposed of by those who consume wealth, cater to consumption of wealth, or otherwise handle the wealth when once produced, and if only a small part goes to assist the wealth-producers, it is no wonder that competition in every business is great.

We act like a farmer who spends the bulk of his capital in improving and decorating his reaping-machines and leaves insufficient for preparing the ground and putting in the seed.

Many English producers, especially manufacturers, who have had an opportunity of seeing what great facilities their French competitors enjoy from their bankers, understand well how handicapped they are in this respect. The extraordinary quickness with which France has several times during this century recovered from the greatest political and financial disasters is accounted for by the fact that the bulk of the wealth of the country is applied to production. Besides, it is not possible that the French nation could have withstood so long the outrageous Protective system under which it suffers if it had not the great advantages which its banking system affords.

The diversion of the working capital of the country from the interests of production causes many serious evils, of which we shall point out only a few of the most evident— viz. : the increase of the number of work-seekers, and decrease of the number of work-givers ; difficulty on the part of capitalists to find safe and lucrative investments ; despotism of capital ; the existence of an army of oppressive and pernicious middlemen ; class hatred ; socialistic tendencies ; advocacy of communistic measures in both imperial and local government, etc.

One of the consequences of our bank law is, as we have already seen, the absence of small and economically useful banks or bank branches throughout the British Empire. Good traditions of the free time linger yet in Scotland ; but in England, Ireland, and the Colonies (where, unfortunately but naturally, the English bank legislation has been more or less copied) the absence of the above-mentioned small banks is conspicuous.

That this is an evil which seems to be evident even to superficial observers is proved by the advocacy in newspapers and periodicals of the introduction of Schulze

Delitzsche Banks, the most miserable and unpractical hybrids between a charitable institution and a bank. Such banks may be an apparently useful makeshifts in a country where economic affairs are managed in so fantastic a manner as in Germany; but in England, where we have some respect for economic facts, we ought to achieve more.

Small note-issuing banks, or bank branches, being forbidden, the way is open to two great sources of misery, improvidence and ruin, i.e., resource to the money-lender and the pawnbroker. These may be indispensable factors in our bad system of co-operation, and we do not blame them; but they are the very worst factors imaginable. The difference between a money-lender and a real bank is, economically speaking, that the money-lender takes advantage of his . client's difficulties to make a profit for himself, finding it to his advantage to increase the difficulties and accelerate the ruin of his client, while the bank (if not vitiated by Government interference) makes its profit by charging a small commission on the profits it facilitates to its clients. The great profusion of the sign of the three golden balls wherever the working-classes congregate, and the large number of money-lenders and *financial agents* in all business centres, is a standing reproach to our legislators, and a constant reminder that we have a banking system void of all economic principles.

The day the Bank Act is repealed the money-lenders will suddenly find that helping people to make profits and fortunes is a more profitable business than ruining them. Money-lenders cannot compete successfully with free banks so far as wealth-producing business is concerned, as we shall make clear in the following chapters.

It is hardly possible to imagine a more effective damper on thrift, enterprise, and an honest desire to work, than the knowledge that the first ' bad times,' or the first mistake, may land one in the hands of the money-lender. The effects of this Damocles' sword are bad in England, but they are even more palpable in Ireland, India, and Egypt, for which latter country we are now responsible. In India and Egypt the money-lender is an institution now indispensable to co-operation. Rational banks are forbidden, but the money-lender who charges 50 per cent. interest and oppresses the people as much as do the respective Governments with all their taxes, and who stands in the way of the prosperity which the taxation presupposes, he is recognised as a useful factor in the production ! The moral suffering which this

3—2

absurd system involves, and the social and political effects it produces, are as bad as the immense economic loss. Any freedom-loving man ought to be able to understand that an Irishman would rather remain poor during the whole of his life than work for the benefit of a money-lender under conditions very little removed from slavery.

And what sane man could be surprised at the hatred and contempt which the ryots of India and the fellahs of Egypt feel for a civilization which cannot suggest any better way of solving such a simple problem as the division of labour than by usury!

That Canada owes all its financial depression and slowness in development to the absence of sound principle in its financial legislation, is denied by no one who understands anything of political economy.

In every new colony we have observed a phenomenon rather puzzling to most people. When the stream of emigration is first directed to a new country, progress is considerable, business good, labour in demand, and profits easy. But when there arises a community with a bank law of the usual type, a change for the worse at once sets in. In the very countries where Nature stores inexhaustible natural riches, and where the scope for labour is almost endless, we find scarcity of life's necessaries and comforts, and scarcity of work!

The cause is, of course, that the vicious banking system upsets all calculation and destroys the motive for work, viz., the profit. It costs the people more to produce and ship their goods than they can get for them, and production must then decline.

The loss of trade which results to England from the miserable state of her chief customers, her colonies, must be enormous, and is due to the bank laws.

Such are the principal effects of our absurd bank legislation, and it is natural that sound logic will trace most of our national evils to this cause. We have prepared and perfected most wonderfully all the wheels in the clockwork of free co-operation; but we have foolishly nailed the pendulum to the wall, from fear that it might swing irregularly, and we are puzzled because our beautiful mechanism will not work. When the pendulum is free the clock will go to great perfection; or, to drop the metaphor, when we have completed our Free Trade system by making banking free, we shall for the first time reap the full benefit of all the improvements we have accomplished during many centuries.

VI.

FREE NOTES THE RATIONAL MEDIUM OF EXCHANGE.

IF we are to re-organize our system of co-operation in accordance with sound theory and reasonable principles, instead of blindly following the rules which our forefathers, in complete ignorance of the subject, laid down, we shall have to choose between two rational systems, namely, complete State management on the one hand and complete freedom of competition, regulated by supply and demand, on the other.

Our present system is a blending, or rather confusion of these two, and like most hybrid systems, it has the faults of both with the advantages of neither. Any change beyond that of mere form must therefore take us nearer to one of the above two rational systems.

Just now we are gravitating towards entire State management, or, to call it by its real name, socialism. We are urged from all sides to take deliberate steps down the inclined plane which leads to it. Now it is a well known fact that State interference is a remedy which has a strong tendency to be required in a larger measure the more it is applied. If, for instance, we were to try to mitigate one of the evils resulting from State interference with co-operation, viz., the bad housing of the poor, by more State interference, and build dwellings at the expense of the State, we should, firstly, check private building through State competition, and, secondly, increase the number of houseless poor through augmented taxation, thus rendering the necessity for State building more urgent than before. Each change in the direction of increased State management is therefore a telling step towards Socialism.

Though the economic circumstances of the country are such as to cause many sincere philanthropists to lean towards socialistic measures, we think that Englishmen in general are almost instinctively averse to the socialistic form of co-operation. We shall therefore not combat here arguments in favour of socialism, but content ourselves with pointing out that in economic respects socialism would be a failure. It would deprive work, daring, invention, enterprise, and even self-control of their most powerful incite-

ments; it would have many of the economic defects of
slavery and despotism; and the absence of individual
liberty which it involves would probably lead to loss of
national independence.

In spite, then, of the clamour of the moment, we may, for
the above reasons, reject any reform in our system of co-
operation which would take us nearer to entire State
management, as a step in the wrong direction. Any
desirable improvement must therefore be found in the
direction of free competition, with maintenance of individual property.

Our task is thus reduced to stating the reply to the
following question: What system of co-operation is the
best; general prosperity being the object, and respect for
individual property and individual freedom being the condition?

In replying to this question, it will be conducive to
clearness to give the entire reasoning which leads to the
conclusion that entirely free banking is the best and only
rational mode of free (not State managed) co-operation.

This cannot be done without a slight and partial recapi-
tulation, for which no other apology will be required.

Our globe produces, or could easily be made to produce,
a thousand times more material for life's necessities, comforts, and even luxuries, than the human race now
consume.

Work is required to make this natural wealth available.
Human beings can exist, and even enjoy life, by working
isolated or associated only in families and tribes; but their
work is hard, and their life rough and full of dangers.

Co-operation on a wide scale is the indispensable condition for civilization, wealth, comfort, happiness, and progress. The greater and easier the co-operation, the greater
the general wealth and happiness. When individual
property is to be maintained, co-operation can be carried on
only by exchange. Facility of exchange is therefore the
first condition to the increase of wealth. Exchange necessarily implies valuation. Direct valuation of goods by any
other goods is slow, difficult, and inexact. A general
value measurer, such as gold is for us now, is therefore of
the greatest importance. The value measurer is such only
in that it is the most desirable and safest medium of exchange.

But we have seen in Chapters I. and IV. that only a
small part of the exchange of a busy place or country can

bo effected directly by the medium of tho value measurer, gold, and that its temporary presence in increased quantity has a destructive influence on production by raising cost.

For extension of business other mediums of exchange must be found, which can do the work of coin without limitation as to supply, and considering the state of society it is highly desirable that the work should be done in the same simple way as coin does it. Coin, the value measurer and the ideal medium of exchange, is in general demand, not because it is consumed, but because it can easily be exchanged for goods or services. Coin in a man's possession is then a power over a certain amount of goods or services, or in other words evidence of certain rights respected by all. It can therefore be superseded in its function by other evidence of rights, while it retains its function of value measurer in all exchanges. Such evidences of rights would then become mediums of exchange. For clearness' sake we will call such mediums of exchange as are not coin 'instruments of credit.' We use here the word credit, of course, in its economic sense, meaning thereby not so much deferred payment as the power of purchasing goods and services, valued in coin, and proved by some stamped, written, printed, spoken, or understood evidence.

It now has to be determined which of the known credit instruments is the most important as an auxiliary medium of exchange, or the one which is most suitable to replace coin and assist it in its function as a medium of exchange without interfering with its function as a value measurer. Coin being the ideal medium of exchange understood by and within the reach of all, and therefore of very extensive use in our productive trades, where want of commercial training and of sufficient means render many of the other credit instruments inapplicable, it is necessary that the credit instrument which we select as a substitute for coin should possess as many as possible of the advantages of coin without its disadvantages.

To enable us to examine more easily the known instruments of credit, we arrange them in the following scale:

1.	2.	3.	4.	5.	6.	7.
Coin.	State bank-notes.	State superintended notes.	Free notes.	Cheques.	Bills.	Accounts current.

They have been thus placed in order according to their degree of similarity with coin. We will examine them, beginning with the last, viz., No. 7, Accounts current.

An amount credited in the ledger of a bank or good commercial firm will buy goods and services to the same amount in coin. Accounts current will then, where they exist, render the same services as coin. A very large business is daily transacted all over the world with no other medium than accounts. They have not the defects of coin, regarded as a medium of exchange, inasmuch as the increased use of them will not directly affect prices of goods as increased presence of coin does. Large amounts may be credited and debited in merchants' books any number of times without affecting the value of coin. Also, for large businesses accounts current are a cheaper medium of exchange than coin, and the possible use of such a system may be called unlimited.

Such are the advantages of accounts current over coin. These advantages are very important. But accounts can replace coin only in certain kinds of transactions between certain classes of people. They cannot be used as the general substitute for coin which we are in want of; they are not a portable and easily transferable evidence of credit; they can be used only by people of a certain commercial standing; they can effect exchanges only between people known to each other as solvent and honest; and they are not suitable for small transactions amongst the general public.

Let us now examine No. 5, Cheques, and No. 6, Bills. These have similar advantages, though to a less degree, to those we have described as belonging to accounts current, and are also free from the disadvantages attached to coin; besides which they are portable and transferable. But at the same time they have all the restrictions to their use that accounts have, and would therefore not well replace coin.

No. 4, Free notes, offer the same kind of facilities as accounts current. They are cheap, easily procurable in the exact amount wanted, and at the same time they can be handled in exactly the same way as coin. They can be used by all who can use coin; they are transferable by simple exchange, etc. If, besides, they are free from those disadvantages which coin has as a medium of exchange— a fact which we shall prove in the following chapter—free notes have then similar advantages to those of *all* the other mediums of exchange without having *any* of their defects.

That No. 3, State superintended notes, and No. 2, State Bank notes, have all the disadvantages which coin has as a medium of exchange, we shall prove hereafter.

If we now return to the scale on page 39, and read over the different credit instruments from right to left, we find that the advantages fully present in No. 7 are present in some form in Nos. 6, 5, and 4, but not at all in 3, 2, or 1.

If we proceed from left to right we find that the advantages realized in No. 1 (coin) are present in Nos. 2, 3, and 4, but not in 5, 6, or 7, or, in other words, that the disadvantages of coin stop at No. 3, and the disadvantages of accounts current stop at No. 5. No. 4 (Free notes) thus stands out prominently as possessing all the advantages and being free from the disadvantages of all other instruments of credit.

We thus come to the conclusion that free notes are the perfection of all credit instruments, and the only one which can replace coin advantageously. The other credit instruments are good and useful in their places, but none of them can prove an adequate sole substitute for coin regarded as a medium of exchange.

It remains yet to prove what we have so far presupposed —namely, that State Bank notes and State superintended notes are no improvement on coin, but have all its disadvantages, and that free notes have, as a medium of exchange, none of the disadvantages of coin.

As these facts are very important links in the chain of our reasoning, and as they are ignored by all who have legislated for banking, and, as far as we know, by all who have written on the subject, we shall devote a separate chapter to them.

<hr>

VII.

THE EFFECT OF STATE SUPERVISION OVER NOTE ISSUING.

When redeemable State Bank notes are issued they do not increase the quantity of the circulating mediums of exchange in the country, for the reason that gold leaves the country in exact proportion to the issue of the notes, everything else remaining unchanged.

There is no lack of proof drawn from experience, for this economic fact, and its explanation is as follows. A quantity of State Bank notes known to be safe and redeemable at sight would—being equivalent to coin—have the whole country for their market; when issued they would buy some kind of goods or services; a scarcity of this kind of goods or services would be caused, and would be filled from other places than that in which the notes were first issued. Capital employed in buying services having a tendency to become invested in goods for immediate consumption, we need speak here only of goods. If the goods purchased for the new notes came from abroad, a quantity of gold corresponding to the issued notes would leave the country at once in payment for this extra import, as the notes could not be used for payments out of the country. We suppose here, of course, an isolated, ideal transaction; in reality the phenomenon would be complicated by variations in the rate of exchange, and a great number of other transactions; but the final result would always be that the issued notes would take the place of a corresponding quantity of gold, which would remain abroad. If, on the other hand, the goods absorbed in the first instance were home products, the home production would first increase; everything else remaining the same, the consumption of raw material, provisions, etc., would increase and wages rise. The increased activity in one place would soon spread, and the advance in prices would permeate the whole country, if the first cause, that is, the quantity of issued State Bank notes, was sufficiently important. An advance in prices all over the country means necessarily less export, and more import : the difference would be paid in gold corresponding to the quantity of the issued notes. (In reality the gold might not actually be paid; it might be kept back from intended gold shipments to the country, etc., but the actual result would be so much less gold in the market than would have been there if the supposed extra issue of State Bank notes had not taken place.) We find, then, that the issue of State Bank notes affects the country in exactly the same way as imported gold, described in Chap. IV. The advantage from State Bank notes is then limited to the interest saved on the quantity of gold they replace—a very small advantage indeed, and more than counterbalanced by the deterioration of the value measurer, and the insecurity which results from increasing the promises to pay while still the gold is banished. Strange to say, this so-called advantage of saving the interest of the replaced gold is the only one mentioned by

most writers on banking as resulting from all kinds of
notes. They are quite right so far as State Bank notes are
concerned, but it is strange that the effects of free banking
in Scotland did not suggest to them the vital importance
of free bank-notes.

It has been said that State Bank notes have proved very
useful, at least when first introduced, as may be gathered
from the history of banking in several countries. But the
fact is that it was not the notes which caused the noticed
improvement, but the simultaneous extension of banking,
which could have been carried on very well without notes,
and very much better with free notes.

It may further be urged that when State Bank notes are
issued they cause an increase in business, and thereby
enable the market to carry increased mediums of exchange.
Our reply to this is that the increase of activity is entirely
temporary, and lasts only during the interval necessary to
raise prices high enough to check production and export,
and thus send the gold out. When the gold has left the
country, and the corresponding capital is consumed, things
turn out much the same as before, if not worse by reaction.

Private notes supervised by the State are the worst kind
of notes. The State supervision is either efficient enough
to make the note safe in the estimation of the people, or it
is insufficient, only lending an empty prestige to the notes,
and giving the people a delusive guarantee. The latter
kind of supervision would be an act of deception on the
part of the Government, and though it has been practised
more than once, we may consider it obsolete. It remains
to examine how the notes of private banks made, relatively
speaking, safe by law would affect the trade of the country.

In the first place they would affect the trade of the
country as coin does, because the Government having
undertaken to look after the security, the people would
make no distinction between the notes of the different
banks, but cause them to circulate indiscriminately all
over the country. Excess of issue could only be discerned,
therefore, when the reaction had fully developed, that is,
after production and export had been seriously affected.
Superintended notes being equal to coin in their financial
and economic effects would cause banking to take the
objectionable form of coin lending, inducing none of the
delicate and intelligent handling so conducive to prosperity,
which results naturally from free banking, or even from the
French banking method. Then we find that State super-

vised banks cannot achieve the public object for which they are established, namely, to augment the mediums of exchange. They cannot make any considerable use of their right of note issue except when they can secure a sufficient gold reserve, and when the general market of the country is in a condition to carry an increased quantity of notes. But these conditions are fulfilled only when business is flourishing, and when prices are favourable to production and export, or in other words, just when there is enough coin and coin notes in circulation, but not too much to send prices up and hamper export. Such periods are the opportunities of these banks, and they naturally take advantage of them to issue as much of their notes as they can force into the market. The notes drive the gold out of the country, and its scarcity soon becomes embarrassing, because it is wanted to pay for the increased import inflated by great consumption, unwise production, and artificial flush times. When the circulation of the notes is thus at its height, and a great need for them is developed, the banks find it absolutely necessary, in consequence of the increasing scarcity of gold, to withdraw their notes as quickly as possible, and a crisis is created which lasts until prices have again dropped sufficiently to tempt those who have means left to again start production and export. Thus these banks increase enormously the circulating mediums of exchange when such an increase is undesirable, and withdraw them when the demand for them is greatest. In countries where this absurd system is in vogue the people pay dearly for any short period of prosperity which they can snatch through exceptional favourable circumstances, and such periods are infrequent.

The notes being taken indiscriminately all over the country, no supervised bank has any control over the surrounding market, or what ought to be its own market. Such banks do not care to have a merely local control, the whole country being their market. The interest of each is to circulate its notes as far from the bank as possible, and liberal terms are given to distant customers. A more effective way of gorging the country with notes could hardly be imagined, and the country is full of them to overflowing; the notes are always in excess of the quantity compatible with sound business.

The result of course is that prices are kept as high as possible, production as dear and as small as possible, work scarce as possible, and business as unprofitable as possible.

Excessive import and a tendency towards foreign indebtedness are apt to become chronic amongst people who thus deliberately corrupt their value measurer, introduce base paper coinage, and bring on themselves all the evils of gold-producing countries without being able to produce an ounce of gold.

Free notes have no such effects on the economy of the country where they are circulating. The fundamental reason for this is that, free from all State supervision, they never acquire the attributes of coin. In whatever form they may be issued, and in whatever way they may be handled, they always remain credit instruments, with no other effect on the market than cheques would have. While State supervised notes are coin—bad paper coin—free notes are cheques. They can be used as coin wheresoever coin can be used: they do not produce the effect of coin on production and export, but accomplish fully the objects of cheques in the same way as cheques.

To well grasp this argument minute investigation is necessary. We must first inquire into the nature of free bank notes. The general impression is that as soon as everybody in this empire is permitted to issue notes payable to bearer on demand—or what is generally called bank notes—everybody would set about issuing notes, everybody would soon have too many notes out, everybody would stop payment, and everybody would be ruined.

As a matter of fact, everybody would not, and could not, issue notes ; because the following conditions are, by force of circumstances, attached to free note-issuing :

First Condition.—The issuer of free notes must be of good standing, and have ample means.

When all State interference disappears, notes will have to circulate entirely on their own merit. Who would, under such circumstances, take an unknown man's or a poor man's notes as cash ? Just as many as would now take an unknown or poor man's I O U as cash.

A man of small means would find note-issuing a most difficult, not to say impossible, way of raising capital. He would gain his object much sooner, and with far less expense, through bills or promissory notes at fixed due dates, or any other instrument of credit. And if a poor man, by some chance, did get some one to take his notes, would they not be presented for payment at once, and then where would the issuer's advantage be ? It is, then, out of the

question that anyone except firms and companies of good
standing would ever attempt to issue notes ?

*Second Condition.—Notes can be issued only by carrying
on a banking business.*

The reasons for this are as simple as they are conclusive.
If free notes were issued in any other way, they would be
presented for payment at once. If notes are not lent nor
used for discounting, they can only be given away as presents, or used as payment for goods or services. If a rich
man were to issue notes for these two latter purposes, they
would be taken out of politeness ; but they would at once
either be presented for payment, or passed through banks
and clearing-houses as cheques. No one would have any
interest in circulating them, and everywhere they would be
subject to a commission, if they were received at all, which
would be quite enough to send them home very soon. But
even if a rich man not carrying on a banking business *could*
succeed in circulating a quantity of notes, it would be about
the last thing he would desire to do. There is hardly any
greater business nuisance imaginable for a rich man than
to have small amounts coming due constantly and irregularly. Why should he expose himself to this, when he can
buy largely on long, fixed credit, pay with cheques on his
banker, or secure his supply in many other ways less expensive, troublesome, and annoying than note-issuing ? Banking
is therefore the only possible way, and the only advantageous
way, of issuing notes.

*Third Condition.—The issuing banker must issue his
notes only through customers carrying on business in the
locality where the notes are issued.*

When banking is entirely free, notes will not circulate
beyond the neighbourhood of the issuing office—that is,
where the bank is well known. Banks being numerous,
under a free system the people will have to look at the
notes before they take them as cash, and they will very
soon adopt the habit of refusing all notes they are not
accustomed to. Every banker will, to defend his own
market, treat other banks' notes as cheques, and charge a
commission on them. These and many other circumstances
will prevent the notes from leaving their natural market.
Even in England, where note-issuing is monopolized by
some few banks of unquestionable standing, where Government watches over a strictly limited issue, and where, consequently, there are fewer causes to keep the private notes
within their respective markets, these notes circulate only

round the banks of issue. At some distance from the issuing office few of the notes are found, and many an Englishman has never seen an English private bank-note, although there are now in England fourteen note-issuing banks, besides the Bank of England.

If, therefore, a free note-issuing banker were to lend his notes to people outside his own market, they would all come back at once, either to be exchanged for gold, or as payments which would otherwise have brought him gold. Such a transaction would diminish the banker's metallic cash, and it would be useless to send away the notes at all. If a banker would lend capital to customers outside his natural market, he would not send his notes, as they might come back all in a lump, and cause him some inconvenience ; he would send gold, a cheque, a draft on some other bank, or some such document. If he wants his notes to circulate, he must pay them out in the only place where they have a chance of staying—namely, his own market.

Fourth Condition.—The free issuing banker must work only with people whose business consists in furthering production or export from the district.

If an issuing banker lends his notes to a customer, the latter will buy goods with them, and consume the goods ; a scarcity of this kind of goods is thereby caused, and is filled from other markets, without countervailing export ; the import must be paid for, but as the notes are not acceptable outside the market, they must be exchanged for gold or gold's equivalent (a draft on some one outside the market) before the payment can be made. Lending his notes to consumers amounts, then, for the issuing banker, to the same as lending his gold. He might lend his gold to consumers, but he would not thereby circulate his notes.

Fifth Condition.—The issuing banker must endeavour to work only with people who have a profit on their business.

If the producers or exporters to whom the free notes are lent spend more on their goods than they obtain for them when sent out of the market, they cause a deficiency of goods exactly as a consumer would do. A losing production is, economically speaking, a consumption pure and simple. The issuing banker must avoid unsuccessful producers or exporters on the same grounds as he would consumers.

Such are the chief conditions which the force of circumstances imposes on bankers who wish to create a note circulation. Anyone who takes the trouble to study the

matter will find that these conditions are safer and much
more to the purpose than any conditions or regulations
which the Government could impose.

Having now gained some insight into the nature of free
notes, it will be possible to grasp thoroughly the important
fact that free notes, as we have described them, will not
affect the country in the same way as the use of coin or
State-supervised notes.

Every issuing banker must keep a certain quantity of
gold in stock to meet such quantities of notes as are likely
to be presented for payment. If a banker carries on his
business in such a way as to leave himself short of coin, he
may be obliged to stop payment, even though only tempo-
rarily and though he be wealthy, and thereby lose his credit,
his business, his connection, and the result of all his work.
He must, therefore, carefully avoid over-issuing.

But, on the other hand, the more notes he can keep in
circulation, the larger is his profit through interest on the
notes, and through the increased turn-over.

Self-preservation on one side, and the desire for profit on
the other, thus determine the limits of a banker's issue.

Free notes produce—but, note it well, only within their
own market—the same effect as coin would produce circulated through the same channels. It is the important fact
that the effect of free notes is necessarily limited to their
own market, which gives them, as a medium of exchange,
the great superiority over coin. We have already given
the reasons why the free notes do not leave their own
market.

If, therefore, the banker issues in excess, the notes do not
spread further in the country, but come back to be exchanged for gold, which can and does leave the district.
We shall explain why. An issuing banker works, as we
have seen, only with producers or exporters (from the district). When the customer of the bank gets the notes, he
spends them in raw material, tools, wages, etc. ; an extra
import into the district follows, and there is a balance
against the market in which the bank works, which may be
paid in gold, or left to be paid by the produced goods. The
fact that the notes come into the market through the
channel of production causes at once an increased activity ;
many people buy and sell more, many produce more, and
many consume more, and more notes are therefore required.
Thus the free notes improve their own market, and make
it more fit for their own circulation. When the note-issuing

is extended, it tends to increase the import, but this import is paid for by the fresh products, and not in gold. As the producers and exporters have a profit on their goods, and the workpeople may save something out of their wages, the new products have a higher value than those which have been consumed in their production. Consequently, there remains a balance in favour of the market of the issuing bank, and gold has a tendency to flow into that market rather than to leave it. The balance will be added to the working capital of the district, and the prosperity will be permanently increased.

Should the banker now send out too many notes, prices would advance, because too many would compete in buying the products of the district and the services of the people. Production would then have to stop, or be carried on at a loss. As we have seen, the result would in either case be the same—gold would leave the market. The chief gold stock is with the banker, and he has to part with it, obtaining his notes in return. A drain on the gold stock is a danger and great inconvenience to the banker, and he will, therefore, always avoid over-issuing. He can easily do this. His metallic cash always tells him the exact state of the market, and with such a sure guide the banker soon learns to avoid not only runs, but all increase in the return of notes as compared with issue. He cannot help but find out by experience that any attempt to flood his market with notes is bound to bring a reaction which will reduce his circulation, and that his only way of increasing his note circulation is to improve the condition of his market; this he can do by choosing the best producers as his customers, by giving his support to all promising enterprises, and avoiding over-issuing. If the banker pays attention to the indication of his metallic cash, he can easily keep his market in a steady, progressive state.

With coin and State supervised notes no such natural regulations exist. The whole country is always becoming over-supplied with coin-notes—we mean over-supplied in proportion to the business doing—and the whole market is constantly in a state which requires part of the circulating value-measurer to be withdrawn, and only issued gradually through the channels of production, in proportion to the improvement in the market. But there is no one to do this delicate work. A State bank or any centre of issue or gold-storing, can only act when the gold begins to leave the country—that is, when the mischief is done, when produc-

4

tion is checked, when foreign competition has prevailed, when time, capital, trade, and connection are lost. Besides, there may be cases when all the trades of the country are suffering from over-inflation of prices through excess of issue while some political or some great external cause keeps up the gold-supply and still encourages a large issue. The state of the metallic cash of a national bank is not so true an indication of the condition of trade in the country as the private banker's metallic cash is of the state of his smaller market. The crisis towards which a country deprived of free banking is naturally drifting when no exceptional cause of prosperity is at work is in a free banking country prevented, all the causes of it being carefully removed in detail by the bankers. The normal state of a free-banking country is, therefore, one of steady, uninterrupted progress; while the country with State-supervised notes has a tendency to drift towards economic crises, and experiences only short and infrequent periods of that kind of prosperity which, in reality, is only the reaction from extreme depression, and is produced by enormous sacrifice of capital and great suffering amongst the people.

Such is the difference between State-supervised notes, adopted by every civilized country and recommended by most writers on banking, and free notes, the use of which is forbidden by law all over the civilized world.

VIII.

OBJECTIONS TO FREE BANKING REFUTED.

OF all the prejudices in the commercial world, that against free banking is probably the strongest and certainly the most general. The objections put forward against it are many and various. And yet these objections are all based on mere supposition, because no fact exists or has existed in any country at any time which can be cited in defence of them; and the prejudice is unreasonable and unreasoning, being at variance with all sound political economy. Almost every economic and commercial incident in the world directly or indirectly illustrates the correctness of the theories in favour of free banking, or the principles on which they are founded.

But, after all, the prejudice against free banking is both pardonable and easily explained. During hundreds of years bank-notes have been called 'money,' and the evils which have resulted from bad 'money' have been very great and very numerous. A safe 'currency,' or safe 'money,' is therefore considered as the first result which a bank law should attain. It is only natural that most people should feel frightened at the idea that everybody in this empire should be allowed to issue bank-notes, or, as it is generally put, to coin paper-money. With such superficial views of the question, it is no wonder that people should at first consider a great number of the objections against free banking as both reasonable and weighty. But after having found in Chapter VI. what stringent conditions free banking imposes on the issuer of notes, and that only well managed banks can attempt such a business, we may dismiss all objections raised against note-issuing by other than bankers as entirely groundless, because it would never be attempted by such. It suffices then to meet the objections raised against free issuing banks or bankers.

It is said that if banking were free, dishonest men could take to banking, secure a large circulation for their notes, and when a large number were out, fail or decamp.

Let us see if such a thing would be likely to occur.

To begin with, it will be necessary for a dishonest banker to have a good name. His real character must remain a secret to all, as a man whose dishonesty was known would find it impossible to circulate his notes. He must also have a considerable capital. We must also suppose that he has perseverance and intelligence enough to work up a considerable business of that sound and healthy kind which alone will circulate notes, because we know by experience that the note circulation is small compared with the business, and that in all banks the proportion of coin and notes to the turn-over of the bank tends to diminish as the business grows. (A good London bank does about $1\frac{1}{2}$ per cent. of its business with cash.)

If we suppose all this, we are still short of a very important factor, namely, a sensible motive for failing or running away. It would pay the dishonest man better to carry on a good business, or to sell it instead of ruining it. But let us, for argument's sake, suppose that there was a motive for dishonesty, and let us see whether he could gain any advantage at all by running away or failing fraudulently. Against the notes he issues he receives no coin, no goods—

simply claims on his customers.   He cannot work his business without a substantial metallic cash reserve, and a great part of that is also in his customers' hands.   Thus his customers have more of his cash than he has of theirs.   If he runs away he cannot take the claims with him.   He might have rediscounted all bills and warrants; but we know that cash accounts are the best means of circulating notes, and he could not discount these.   As under a free system the total of granted cash accounts will always exceed considerably the circulation of notes, we find that even if we suppose a number of highly improbable contingencies the fraud feared is simply *impossible.*

It was not by chance that so few banks failed in Scotland during the 150 years of freedom which preceded the Bank Act of 1844.   The almost complete absence of bank failures is the more conclusive if we consider that during this time the Government committed all sorts of financial absurdities, and caused fearful panics in England ; that times were very troubled, and that the true theories of banking were unknown.

It has further been objected that a banker might begin with an honest note-issuing business, gradually go in for a deposit business, obtain a large amount of deposits, and then decamp.

If such a thing did happen the loss would be caused by the deposit business, and not by the note-issuing.   Deposit banks can easily ruin themselves and thousands of their customers (or shareholders, if they are unlimited), and they may now be carried on by anyone.   Note-issuing, which cannot be put to any bad use, is forbidden by law.   If the two branches were carried on by one bank, such bank would have to be far more cautious and more rational than a bank which does not issue notes.   Note-issuing is therefore a most healthy check on a bank, and tends to keep it straight.   A note circulation would hamper a dishonest or imprudent banker, and he would get rid of it before he took any undue advantage of deposits.   Besides, it is evident that note circulation decreases as deposits increase.   Deposit accounts make other and cheaper instruments of credit possible than notes, such as cheques and bills.   Notes are used in connection with cash accounts, and cheques with deposit accounts.   If a bank doing an issuing business combined with other business were to go wrong, it would be found that the note-issuing had acted as a safeguard for the creditors and shareholders by enforcing moderation, and by precipitating an early disclosure of the true state of affairs.

But let us suppose what would not occur often, namely, that an issuing bank did fail, and even, what is highly improbable, that it failed with as many notes out as its market could carry. Would such a failure be very disastrous? We must, again, remember that under a free system the note circulation is small in proportion to the turn-over of the bank, and that this proportion tends to diminish. At the end of the free period of Scotch banking, the aggregate note circulation of all the Scotch banks was below four millions, and in 1840-1841 it was as low as three millions, while the deposits reached forty millions. The amount which could be lost by note-holders would not only be small, but would be divided over a very great number. Few people now keep in their own hands a large amount of cash, and with more banks still fewer would do so. The amount lost by unpaid notes when an issuing bank failed would therefore be small for each holder; but when a deposit bank fails, thousands may lose their fortunes! Our wonderful Bank Law thus protects our purses; but our fortunes it not only leaves unprotected, but actually undermines.

A great argument of the opponents of free banking is that the working man might be the loser if a free bank failed. Should we then keep the working man in constant poverty in order to protect him against a remote chance of losing a few shillings through a bank failure? Compared with such reasoning it would be wisdom to recommend the cessation of all railway traffic for fear of accidents. Such arguments do not require refutation. We may, however, point out that the working man has the right to refuse any note he may suspect, or he may have it endorsed by the person who pays it to him; that few working men would keep even a full week's wages in notes, as it is either consumed or placed in a savings bank; and, finally, that all the holders of cash accounts in the failing bank would be entitled to pay their debt to the bank in notes, and would therefore be able to cash the notes in the hands of others after the bank had failed. This they would probably be willing to do at a small discount. The risk of the working man would thus be imperceptibly small, or something like a small discount, or a few shillings once perhaps in a century.

Another objection raised is that when many banks are allowed to issue notes, ignorant people who cannot distinguish the notes of one bank from those of another may be made to accept valueless paper in payment.

Such a thing has happened, though seldom, in countries where the Government supervise the banks, and where all notes circulate indiscriminately, and where consequently no one notices what bank has issued the notes received ; but in a country where it is generally known that the Government has nothing to do with the notes, only simpletons could be taken in by papers resembling notes. Even carefully-executed forged notes could have no chance of a circulation that would repay the forger. As the free notes do not circulate all over the country like Government notes, but have a limited market, run in fixed channels and reappear often in the banks, forged ones could more quickly be detected and traced to their origin than forged Government supervised notes. In any case it would always be easier to forge cheques and to deceive by cheques ; but no one dreams of prohibiting cheques because not only stupid people but a great many clever people are taken in by them !

It has been said that if an issuing bank were to stop payment, there would be a run on all the other issuing banks, and a general panic might follow.

There is no experience to justify such fear, nor can a reasonable ground be given. Under a free system centralization disappears, and each bank stands more independently of other banks than under any other system. To arrive at having a good note-circulation, a bank must be very useful to its market, and will therefore be popular. All who derive advantage from the bank will do their best to prevent a run, and all the cash-account customers will not only have a special reason for protecting the bank, but will have great power to do so, as they can without any risk to themselves cash notes up to the amount of their own balance. As note-issuing is not a business likely to bring about the failure of a bank with a large circulation, there would be a special reason for each failure, which would be generally known ; and as each bank would be well known on its market, only those banks would be affected by a failure which had suffered from the same cause.

Some people seem to fear that in case of complete absence of State regulation, a great quantity of very small notes would be issued, and that these would drive all the silver out of the country and generally prove a great nuisance.

It must be remembered that the smaller the amount represented by each note, the smaller is the profit on the issue. It costs as much to print, number, check, and issue a note for five shillings as one for a hundred pounds. The issuing bank would, therefore, not send out more small notes than the market could hold regularly. Whether small notes would supersede silver or not would of course depend on the public. If there existed any dislike to notes under a certain amount, such notes would come back too frequently to give the bank any profit. They would oblige the banker to keep a silver cash reserve as well as a gold one, for if he at any time refused to oblige his customers or even outsiders with silver, his small notes would not circulate at all. Thus the public would have it in their power to decide the minimum amount at which a note becomes a nuisance. In busy centres no small notes would pay, and would probably not be issued ; but in outlying, poor, and isolated districts, small bankers might be able to make one shilling notes pay, and in such places, where change is scarce, no one would object to them.

Many countries have had State bank notes of very small amounts, and instead of proving a nuisance they were found very convenient for all kinds of business requiring a great quantity of change, as they weighed very little and could be easily carried or sent in parcels and letters. An amount in small notes would go in a pocket-book, while the same amount in silver would be a burden. There was only one objection to these small notes ; being State notes they had a very wide and protracted circulation, and were only renewed when they happened to be paid into the State bank. They therefore became dirty and ragged. But free private notes would make their appearance frequently in the bank, and could easily be renewed.

Of the objections against free banking which have come under our notice, these seem the most sensible.

IX.

FORECAST OF RESULTS OF FREE BANKING IN ENGLAND.

IF free trade in banking were introduced now throughout the British Empire it would in a short time open a period of growing prosperity, and close a term of that normal depression which is inseparable from hampered division of labour, and which becomes intense when, as now, it is not counteracted by some special causes of activity in trade.

The effects of free banking would be great and prompt, because it would enable us for the first time to enjoy the benefit of all modern improvements, up to now neutralized by the absence of rational banking. Co-operation will, when free, benefit enormously from the last fifty years' progress in government, colonization, means of communication, and science. Free banking would, by supplying an unlimited wealth-producing medium of exchange, incapable of being abused, give for the first time to this widespread Empire the greatest development to co-operation compatible with our system of civilization. This is saying much, but it may be interesting to point out here not all of these results —that would be impossible—but the most important of those which can be proved from experience or by deductions from the preceding chapters.

Free banking would cause credit to be cheap and coin to retain its highest value; or, in other words, capital to be supplied to labour at a low rate of interest, and cost of production to remain low. The bulk of the capital of the nation would find its way into the channels of genuine production, in preference to those of consumption, speculation, and spurious business.

The intelligence existing amongst the lower middle and working classes, now often wasted, would be largely utilized, as the banks would derive more profit from intelligent customers than from rich ones.

The cash credit system would be adopted, as it was in Scotland, by all the issuing banks wherever the presence of natural raw material, large population, or any other facilities for business might exist. The number of work givers would thereby be greatly increased, and a great many people would get a start in life.

Wages would be high and living cheap, and the working classes would be well off.

Production would be large, cleverly managed, and profitable.

Consumption would be in proportion.

Hence large import and corresponding export. Consequently Commerce would be flourishing and professions well paid.

The complaint of 'no work to do' would cease. So long as there are men fond of luxuries, pleasure, or refinement, there will be more work in the world than can be done; only it must be allowed to fall into the natural free division.

The strife between capital and labour would cease,

because no labour would bo lost for want of capital. The despotism of capital would collapse, for the capitalist would depend as much on the workers as the workers on the capitalist.

Capital would always bo waiting on work, through tho medium of the banks. An honest and capable man would easily find capital for any paying business, especially for one of production, as tho banks would derive a double profit from any healthy increase of production in their markets.

Capital, though no longer a despot, would find safer and more profitable investment, because the free banks would supply the long missing channels through which it can reach safe and paying production. And through note-issuing the banks could pay good dividends, allow good interest on deposits at long and fixed periods, and still charge a moderate interest on advances.

The great cause of stagnation in business—viz., the great increase of coin for a small increase in production—would disappear, as would consequently the tendency of the cost of production to exceed the price of sale, which tendency must prevail when we overload our own country, where our production is financed, with coin taken from countries which are our natural customers. With free banking no such tendency would exist; firstly, because gold would not be imported, but notes would be used, and we consequently would not lower the price of sale abroad; secondly, because any over-issue would only affect the district of the over-issuing bank, and would be speedily corrected; thirdly, because the notes would go direct to production, and create a demand or a market for themselves, failing which they would be retired before they could raise the cost of production too much for sale and export; fourthly, because with note-issuing banking would pay, even on a small scale and with a small capital, in all places where there is an opening for it, and the humblest producers in even the remotest parts of the country would have the great benefit of banking, after a method superior to that which London has ever had, and would have the chance of carrying on their business as advantageously as the London firms—namely, 98 per cent. by means of banking, and 2 per cent. with coin.

The financial position of the nation would bo safer. Instead of one single gold stock there would be many—namely, one in each bank. The quantity of gold in the country would be smaller than now, compared with the business ; but larger than the actual stock now in the country, the volume of business being so much greater. The gold supply would not fluctuate and produce sudden changes in the markets as it does now. It would grow steadily, but only in small proportion to the business. A gold panic could hardly be possible, while now one might set in at the end of every period of depression.

Honesty, thrift, sobriety, and other virtues would be greatly encouraged, as they would be indispensable conditions for a good cash account. The English would find, as the Scotch found before 1844, a good character to be a discountable capital which would secure them cash for a start in life.

When the supply of capital is decentralized, and independent business centres (banks) established all over the country, the tendency of labour to centralize in the large towns will be much less, if it does not disappear.

No one would lose by the free banking reform. The Bank of England would have to give up an absurd monopoly which even some of the directors, if we are well informed, consider of very questionable value. The Bank of England would give up the monopoly of note-issuing, but keep all its other privileges, and certainly its worldwide prestige, and it would gain its *freedom.* Its notes would, of course, cease to be legal tenders. The value of freedom to a bank of such a position and such a prestige would be very great. The loss of the monopoly would not diminish but increase its circulation, and would be a gain in every way, because a monopoly which undermines the business of the whole empire must be very disadvantageous to its chief bank. The bank reform would therefore cause no loss to the Bank of England. Nor would it in any way harm any other bank. The large banks would probably not try to circulate notes, as their connection is already above this primitive instrument of credit ; but they would probably have many note-issuing branches for customers. Their business would thereby extend considerably, and the extension would be very safe, as all papers coming through these banks would have the endorsements of the latter.

The fact that no one would lose anything, and that most people would gain considerably by free banking, would soon induce other nations to follow England's example. They have not done so with regard to Free Trade, because the protected people are supposed to lose something through Free Trade, and because the reform has not freed

England from periods of depression in trade. It will be easier for America and the Continent to follow the lead of England in banking than in Free Trade.

And those countries which adopt free banking will have taken an important step towards Free Trade, because the only sensible arguments in favour of Protection are based on two fallacies which free banking will expose—namely, that the various protected nations have no work to do and that they lack capital.

Every country which adopts free banking will very much increase its prosperity, and consequently its trade with England. Should no country follow England's example, England would be the leading country in production, and have only a small and weak competition to contend with.

Emigration would not require State assistance. The right people would go out with sufficient means, intelligent plans, and with a direct view to develop the business of their friends at home.

The effects of free banking will be very striking in most of our colonies. In such as Canada, Australia, the Cape, and New Zealand, the immense store of natural wealth in virgin soil could be won freely, because the economic dead lock which is now established by law, and which tends to raise the cost of production above the price of sale, would disappear.

As no reasons can be given why free banking should not do for Ireland what it did for Scotland, we shall here devote a page to free banking in Scotland and its effect.

The prejudice against free banking is so strong and so general that it would probably be useless for a long time yet to try to overcome it by logic alone. But a hundred and fifty years of experience with extraordinary success, which cannot be explained away, ought to go a long way towards convincing a practical people like the English. All writers on the subject agree in upholding the Scotch banking system as it was before 1844 as the perfection of banking, though they never recommend its acceptance except with such modifications as would change its nature altogether.

During nearly a century and a half banking was free in Scotland, if we except some small prohibitions solicited by some of the large banks in a fit of jealousy. Banking was free, not because the legislators understood the vital importance of such freedom, but because no one thought of making a Bank Law.

When in 1844 rational banking was sacrificed in Scotland

for uniformity's sake, no one had a word to say against the
banks; on the contrary, only praise was heard. But unfortunately no one could defend the free system as it ought to
have been defended, for the reason that the true theories
of free banking were not known. The Government had
theories, such as they were, but the friends of free banking
had none, and were beaten.

Walter Scott, though no economist, saw that an injustice
was being done to Scotland, and wanted to know ' why the
Scotch should be forced to take the medicine when it was
the English who were sick ?' The great praise which so
many English and foreign writers lavish on the Scotch
system, and the glowing descriptions they give of its effects,
are by no means exaggerated. When the first bank was
started in Scotland the country was one of the wildest and
least civilized in Europe, which is saying a good deal when
speaking of the end of the seventeenth century. Manufacturing hardly extended beyond a meagre home supply
of the rudest wares, and agriculture was entirely primitive;
black-mailing and robbery must have been of almost daily
occurrence, judging from the laws enacted in those days;
security for life and property was small, and poverty was
appalling. If we compare the state of Scotland in 1690
with its condition in 1844, we attain an idea of the progress
which had been accomplished. No European country can
show such an extraordinary development during so short a
period. This progress becomes more surprising when we
consider that in Scotland at the beginning of that period
almost everything except banking was obstructive to progress and prosperity, and that the effects of free banking
were not accelerated by the great facilities for co-operation
which modern progress has established.

Communication with other countries was slow and
dangerous; there was very little shipping, no railways, no
canals, only bad roads infested by robbers. There was no
Free Trade, no schools, no police. The country was agitated
by political and religious strife, and for want of anything
better to do for a living many young Scotchmen hired
themselves out as mercenaries on the Continent, dis-
tinguishing themselves through their fierceness and reck-
lessness.

Against all these difficulties free banking won for
Scotland the race of progress between the countries of
Europe. It gave Scotland its model farms, its large and
varied manufactures, its fleets of ships, and forty millions

of deposits in the banks. But it did for Scotland what is worth more than all this; it moulded and educated the Scotch into the best business-men in the world. To free banking they owe thrift, economy, good methods, foresight, and trust in hard work.

And who dares to say that free banking would not produce the same results in Ireland ? It certainly would, and in a very short time, because none of the obstacles to co-operation exist now which existed in Scotland then. Increasing prosperity and thrift will produce contentment. All the advantages the country can derive from its connection with a great, self-governing, and free-trading Empire, will be made manifest to the Irish when they have free banking.

But in no country would the effects of free banking be greater than in India, because in no country are the evils consequent on legally prohibited division of labour greater. The British Parliament has for a long time been legislating for India with a sincere desire to benefit its inhabitants, making its usefulness to England a secondary consideration ; but increasing poverty has, so far, been the result, and will be the result so long as co-operation is not either entirely State managed or entirely free. The poverty of India under English rule threatens to become as proverbial as was its wealth before the conquest. If those foreigners who seem to envy England the possession of this ' brightest jewel of her crown,' and who fancy that the free and self-governing 20,000,000 of Englishmen derive untold riches from wealthy India, and the 250,000,000 of conquered Indians, were to inspect our back streets and slums, they would be surprised to find how little the country of fabulous wealth has benefited its masters.

They would certainly think there must be something very far wrong in our management of Indian affairs. And they would be right. Production of wealth is prohibited by the fact that co-operation is prohibited. The very improvements introduced in India have reduced the productive power of the country. We have abolished slavery, compulsory labour and despotism, and thereby removed important factors in the co-operation of the people, without replacing them by others. Such banking as we allow is of no use to the producers, and they have no medium of exchange but coin.

In countries where such an economy is established the money-lenders are sure to multiply. In India they are considered a time-honoured and indispensable institution, and we have not, in all these years during which they have oppressed the people, found the means to free the country from such a curse.   The result is that about 40 per cent. of the ryots are paupers, and 20 per cent. more are insolvent, misery is on the increase, the beautiful and interesting industries of the country are dying out, and the hopelessness of the suffering people is becoming more and more intense.

. What a change we would create if we allowed free co-operation to do for these 250,000,000 of India what it did for Scotland; if we allowed entirely free organization of division of labour between all these people, and between them and the rest of the empire !

The first result would be that the money-lenders would have to make room for free banks.   The peculiar agrarian system of India would not present any serious obstacles, as the reform would increase the revenue of the landowners, who, moreover, could take an interest in the banks.   The people would obtain their capital at 5 per cent. interest instead of 50 or 60 per cent., and would find their cost of production in more favourable proportion to the price of sale.   The ryot is known to be a reliable payer, not only of his own debts, but also of those of his father and grandfather, and such customers are the right sort for cash accounts in free banks.   In India none of those obstacles exist now which obstructed economic progress in Scotland.   By all the improvements effected under the English rule the country is splendidly prepared to reap the greatest benefit from free banking.   The great increase in production which free banking calls forth had, in Scotland, to be raised under a hard climate, in cheap and rough products, from meagre moorlands, as a new experience.   In India free banking would simply have to revive an ancient prosperity, decayed through want of it, and to facilitate the growth and manufacture of the most valuable products in a warm climate, and from the most suitable soil.   The new prosperity in India would totally eclipse the ancient one, because as a medium of co-operation free banking possesses such considerable advantages over the ancient one, the feudal system.   It is evident that from the very beginning of free banking a healthy change would set in.   With ample mediums of exchange, cheap capital, and naturally low cost of production, the Indian farmer would easily supply his wants and soon have products for sale.   To ease the minds of those who are afflicted with the over-production theory, we may point out that as soon as increased production is in operation in India the consumption would necessarily increase ; that as soon as the cultivator could sell produce he would increase his consumption further.

This increased consumption, which increased production and increased wealth naturally and necessarily involve, would react on European markets ; larger orders would come from India, trade would improve in countries which ship to India, and the consumption of Indian produce would increase. Thus, the improvement in India would improve the European markets, and then again react favourably on India. There would therefore be no over-production, but an end to the under-consumption from which we now suffer, and which appears as over-production to superficial observers. Such reciprocal influences can be noticed arising out of even occasional and ephemeral causes of both good and bad trade. Improved, not to say permanently perfected, co-operation in such an important country as India, is therefore sure to react strongly all over the world, as she would draw her supply from many countries, send her produce in return, and thus increase activity everywhere. England, the great free-trading country, would, of course, obtain the bulk of the increased Indian trade. With sufficient capital (and with free banking every market would have sufficient capital) the products of India will not only increase in quantity, but also in number and variety. All the old industries will leap into fresh life, and, under the free division of labour and free exchange with Europe, prove themselves capable of great development and wide application.

Irrigation will be easily and speedily established wherever it is likely to pay, because useful public enterprises are greatly facilitated by free banking, not only indirectly, but also directly. The Scotch note-circulation facilitated and cheapened the construction of canals in Scotland to a very great extent. The same work executed with imported coin would have increased the expenses and paralyzed industry in a great part of the country during a considerable time after the construction, which is proved by every great public enterprise undertaken with coin as the only medium of exchange.

Prosperity in India would accelerate the civilization of all its races, and the more civilization advances the greater will be the demand for European, and especially for English goods.

Finally, we must express our firm belief that when banking has been allowed to establish itself on a truly economic basis, distrust of the truths of political economy will disappear, as the absence of true theories of banking has alone been the stumbling block of its votaries, and the cause of the sad mistakes and consequent misery which do so much to produce sceptical sneers against 'the dry bones of political economy.' True theories will then be established in perfect harmony with all experience, capable of explaining all the economic phenomena which now puzzle statesmen and business-men. The fundamental theories of political economy will, no doubt, be accepted without further discussion, as reliable facts, by the bulk of the masses in the same way as other scientific facts have been accepted.

If, therefore, rational banking could be introduced throughout the empire, all States which form part of it would arrive at a perfect understanding on all economic questions, and have all their interests parallel. This would no doubt strengthen and perpetuate their bond of union, and give to our empire a hitherto unrivalled power and prosperity.

With Western civilization flourishing in our country and our colonies as it never flourished in any country before, joined to the splendour of ancient empires revived and exceeded in our Eastern possessions, we could prove to the world that prosperity does not bring decay, when it springs, not from degrading slavery, but from a soul-ennobling system of economy in perfect harmony with the natural and moral laws of God.

Elliot Stock, Paternoster Row, London.